ARISE ARJUNA

ARISE ARJUNA

Hinduism and the Modern World

David Frawley
(Vamadeva Shastri)

Voice of India
New Delhi

First Published: 1995
First Reprint: 1997
Second Reprint: 1998
Third Reprint: 2000

ISBN 81-85990-27-1

This book does not pretend to be a historical treatise, neither on India, nor on other civilizations; it only fleetingly uses events and people, in an attempt to go beyond the superficial views that have usually been held on India by many historians.

Published by Voice of India, 2/18, Ansari Road, New Delhi – 110 002 and printed at Rajkamal Electric Press, G.T. Karnal Road, Delhi – 110 033.

Contents

Preface

Over the last few years, I have written a number of articles and essays on current issues in Hinduism. These reflect the social, intellectual and historical issues that are important in Hinduism today. Based upon the suggestions of Hindu friends, I decided to include a number of these articles in one volume so that they can reach a larger audience.

The topics chosen are among the most difficult and controversial, which therefore many people may not want to examine so as not to offend anyone. However, unless we examine these topics I don't think we can arrive at Truth, particularly in this time of world crisis which requires that we examine everything.

This book is intended mainly for an Indian audience, which naturally is going to be more familiar with these issues. Unfortunately there are very few people in the West who understand India or Hinduism enough to understand this book or appreciate its seriousness (I might add a number of Hindus fall in the same category). Westerners have taken up certain spiritual aspects of Indian civilization, like its yogic practices, which they use mainly for their own personal benefit, and seldom concern themselves about the state of the culture and how it has suffered under Western religions, political and materialistic influences.

I have written a number of books on the spiritual side of the Hindu tradition including the Vedas, Vedanta and Tantra, as well as works on Ayurveda and Vedic astrology. I have examined Hinduism as a whole in my book *Sanatana Dharma, The Eternal Tradition of Hinduism*, which is the work most relevant to this current study. *From the River of Heaven, Hindu and Vedic Knowledge for the Modern Age* is also relevant to the present study and outlines the different aspects of Hinduism.

One might wonder therefore why I would concern myself with the cultural or apparently mundane side of Hinduism. Those immersed in Hindu spiritual practices may see no necessity for concerning themselves with these outward issues. However, there is a tradition for such an approach. The ancient sages of India did not confine themselves to the inner teachings only. They made their comments about society and about other religions. They produced various Dharma Sutras or teachings regarding one's conduct in the world. Modern teachers who wrote on social issues include Sri Aurobindo, Swami Vivekananda, Swami Rama Tirtha, and Ganapati Muni who provided the inspiration for what I have attempted. While I certainly don't wish to compare myself to such great personages, the point is that such a tradition is also important and sadly neglected today.

Knowing Sanskrit, travelling widely in India and meeting people of all backgrounds, I have seen the tremendous ignorance and misconceptions (many intentional) that have been created about the role of Hinduism and various Hindu groups even in India. People today rely on second hand information, mainly through the news media or from academic sources, which are generally unsympathetic and inaccurate, and so the picture they get is highly distorted and requires an alternative. Seeing this I have been compelled to speak out.

This book is divided into four areas.

1) Social Issues: primarily the misrepresentation of Hinduism both in India and the West and the need for a Hindu awakening.

2) Religious Issues: the Hindu view of religion, the unity of all religions, and Islam and Christianity from a Hindu perspective. I have devoted more space to Islam as this religion is more inimical

to Hinduism and few people appear willing to really examine it.

3) Historical Issues: particularly the Aryan Invasion theory, and the division of India along north-south lines (the Aryan-Dravidian divide).

4) Cultural Issues: Hinduism relative to the world as a whole, and the value of Hindu culture.

The book has a wide scope of subjects but all are important for understanding India today and show the need for a revival of Hinduism in its true spirit.

I have already examined the ancient history issue in my other books *Gods, Sages and Kings: Vedic Secrets of Ancient Civilization* and in *The Myth of the Aryan Invasion of India*. For this reason I didn't go much into this topic in the present volume though it is relevant.

For Hindus, they may wonder why a Westerner would take interest in these issues. Yet do not Hindus take interest in the affairs of Western culture? Why should it be surprising if those born in the West take interest in Hindu culture, which is one of the oldest and richest in the world?

For this book I would like to thank Dr. B.L. Vashta, who first encouraged me to write along these lines, and to the many other individuals and groups both in India and the United States who have encouraged me to continue, particularly the various publications that have printed my articles, which gave me the confidence to present them to a broader audience. Most of the essays in this book have appeared in article form either in India or in the United States, though a number of them have been greatly revised for the book. These publications include, in the *United States*, *Voice of Asia*, *News-India Times, India Times*, and *Fortunes India*, and in India, the *Organizer*, the *Observer* and *Hindu Vishwa*.

India today unfortunately is still asleep to its real heritage, caught in a deep inertia (tamas), and not yet functioning according to its soul. Yet even in this state of sleep it has produced perhaps the greatest spiritual figures of the twentieth century. For the world to really develop spiritually, which is critical today, India must awaken.

This book is dedicated to the awakening of India, not for the sake of India but for the sake of all humanity in this era of global crisis.

Santa Fe, New Mexico, U.S.A.
December 1994

DAVID FRAWLEY

Section I

Social Issues

1.1
Arise Arjuna

The world, perhaps as usual, is in a state of crisis. Yet unlike previous crises, which were local in nature, the fate of the globe itself is now at stake, not only humanity but all life on Earth is threatened. And in this extremity no nation has yet arisen as a defender of the Truth or spokesperson for the spiritual values of humanity.

The communist nations, after decades of floundering in confusion and corruption, have recently faded with the collapse of their economic structures through perpetual mismanagement. Only the ghost or shadow of communism lingers, while whatever idealism it might have had has been traded in for personal gain. The capitalistic nations strive to maintain their wealth and affluence by exploiting the planet, selfishly consuming the future resources of humanity for their present transient enjoyment. Between new technological wonders and a growing disillusionment with material gains, they move at an uneasy pace.

The underdeveloped or third world falters under exploitation both within and without. Some poor nations slide backwards and carve up their forests to cover short term economic debts to the wealthier countries. Others strain to recover from civil wars fed by arms suppliers from wealthy nations abroad. Yet others are held back by ever growing populations. Famine and disease lurk behind them and prey on them periodically, threatening an all out attack on them in the coming years.

The environment of the planet is reeling under all forms of chemical and industrial pollution and toxic wastes. The Earth is groaning under the weight of human greed and a sense of great planetary changes, climatic and atmospheric appears imminent. Will we be able to continue as we have without something major going wrong in the natural world that we have spoiled? Even if we avoid nuclear war our wastes may prove as lethal as our bombs. Our very medicine itself, which attacks nature, may create the new diseases that will bring down our excessive numbers.

Most of the religions of the world, remnants of a worn medieval mind, struggle between a new secular modernism and an old retarded fundamentalism. Some are still trying to impose their selfish will upon the world and convert the planet to their narrow beliefs— that their's is the only true God, prophet or holy book—as if the acceptance of their religious dogma would somehow solve our human problems. Other religions have compromised and are willing to take a corner in the new material age, bowing down to science as long as they are given a place to continue ruling over their diminished flocks. The great spiritual traditions of the East, Hinduism and Buddhism, do battle with the economic and ideological forces of the West, and the continued shadow of proselytizing Western religions which would still destroy them if they could.

In this struggle we must ask: Where is India? and what role does she have to play? India too struggles with ethnic and religious divisions, with a rapid and often ugly industrialism, with a plundered land and a population out of control. She has her leftists and communists who have twisted her economy and tried to turn the souls of her people against her spiritual heritage. She has her new capitalists ready to make quick money or to ally themselves with the multinational corporations who see India as a great new land to exploit. Where is the soul of India today? Where is her will? She tries to stand for the underdeveloped world, for peace, tolerance, the unity of humanity and respect for all religions. But her direction is not clear. It appears that she can't even discipline herself.

Western secularism, a popular culture caught up in superficial sensation, marks one line of attack against her. Western religions, their exclusive belief systems and their vast resources spent on conversion, attack on the other side. India would like to please everyone. And each group, religious, ethnic or political wants their portion of the country. Separatism reigns, with each group placing its own interests before that of the country as a whole. Everyone wants to take and no one appears willing to give. No one is standing firm to halt this tide of growing sectarianism, selfishness and materialism.

In this battle the modern Hindu does not want to fight, or even to speak out. He accepts the growing secularism and sensationalism coming to his culture from the West, as perhaps necessary for economic growth, or may even see it as progressive, modern and humanitarian. He tolerates in silence the continuing assaults on his culture and its spiritual values from Islamic and Christian forces within his own land. He doesn't like to criticize anyone's religion even if they mock his. He seems weak, in disarray, without confidence or self-esteem. He appears to think that if he ignores these things they will go away in time, but like an infection they continue to spread and poison the country.

The image of the passive Hindu has arisen:

"They do not resist. They do not stand firm. You can take anything you want from them and they won't say anything. They retire in fear, though they hold on to their superstitions. First, they let the Muslims conquer them, then the British. They seldom fought back. They often joined hands with their conquerors and took sides against their own people. Now that they are free they don't know who they are or what to do. They don't know how to rule themselves. They are used to being ruled. They are lucky their country doesn't fall apart. They are looking for a new conqueror, perhaps the economic forces of the West."

Such are the ideas about India that one hears today.

But classical India was never passive and resigned, never gave up without resistance, never gave in without defending Truth in all possible ways. India was a land of great sages and yogis, like Buddha and Shankara, but they were not merely concerned with the Transcendent, they tried to raise up the country and unite it toward a higher goal, turning it into a land where the spiritual life was honored. India was also the land of Rama and Krishna, of great kings and warriors who knew how to rule according to a higher law and protect the spiritual life. India was not a land contracted in itself but open and expansive, spreading its culture of yoga and enlightenment across the seas.

In time the riches of India became the great spoil for all the kings and peoples of the Middle East and Central Asia to assault. Some of these forces gradually made headway into the country. Native dynasties arose in time and drove the invaders out. They did not compromise with outsiders who were inimical to their spiritual heritage. While India's kings gave refuge to the oppressed, they did not bow down before the forces of exploitation. Even the Muslims made dozens of invasions before they ever gained a foothold. The souls who strove so hard, who gave up everything, including their lives, to maintain a land where the spiritual life could flourish should not be forgotten. We must call on them to return again.

Today India as a whole appears to be in the dejection of Arjuna, standing between two great armies before the great and unavoidable battle.

"He has no will to fight. He does not believe in his cause. He would rather let others win than have to challenge or defeat them though he could. It is not simply cowardice that motivates him. It is a sensitive soul that does not delight in conflict."

This is how the spirit of the country appears.

But life is always Kurukshetra. There is always a difficult choice that has to be made. There are always two forces in life, not simply the good and the bad but the ascending force of spiritual growth and the descending force of worldly illusion and division. Nor are the two forces entirely separate. What is one day a spiritual force may in time become a force of ignorance and falsehood once its spirit is lost. These forces cut across humanity and may divide a nation or a family, not to speak of the world itself. To not be willing to face opposition, even from those whom we love if necessary, is to accept the force of decay. This does not mean to be aggressive or violent but to take a stand for the Truth, even if the world turns against us.

"Arise Arjuna! Your's is not a battle at one point of time only. It is for all time. It must be fought over and over again, even for eternity. Truth cannot compromise itself with falsehood. Someone has to hold the limit. If not you, who will it be? And what will you say to your children? What will you bequeath them having surrendered your soul without a struggle?"

What would Arjuna say in these circumstances:

"I will not give in, even one inch to the forces of destruction. If I must be sacrificed, so be it. But I will dedicate my total effort to the fight. Death in the battle is preferable to a life without dignity. The Dharma must be upheld. With adharma there can be no tolerance. We cannot rest until it is completely removed and first it must be stripped from our own hearts."

Such is the spirit that India and the entire world needs today. As a Westerner who has followed Hindu spiritual teachings for over twenty years, returning to the West from India I find some people who delight in the problems of India and others who ignore them. I tell them that to take pleasure in the problems of India is to delight in the sufferings of one's own mother, as India is the mother of the world. India is like the heart center of the planet. That the heart of the globe suffers is not surprising when the head and the hands of the world (Western scientific and technological cultures) are acting without a heart, are living as though their petty pleasures alone were real, anaesthetized to the suffering of the majority of humanity. India may have difficulties but they only reflect those of the world as a whole. Hence my concern with the fate of India though I am not an Indian. The fate of India mirrors the real condition of the world.

A force of inner strength and spiritual guidance for the world is unlikely to come from the countries of the West. The West is too immature, too distorted by the mass media and its culture of self-indulgence. Its spirituality is mixed with a seeking of new sensations and personal achievements, trapped in the body and intellect, and generally far short of any real renunciation or realization. Westerners are more concerned with their own personal, emotional and family problems, not with any greater life of service or spiritual practice. Though there are those in the West who appreciate true spirituality and their number is growing, they are still too small to produce the kind of spiritual leadership that the world needs.

Such a spiritual force is less likely to come from Islamic countries. They are still caught in a karma of violence and oppression, in a religion that is more a political movement to gain worldly power, than any spiritual search. Their religion is dominated by fundamentalism and militancy, not with respect for life and seeking of truth. China, the other great culture of Asia like India, unfortunately will take decades to assimilate communism and develop economically before recovering its more spiritual roots, but it too will arise in time. Its great Buddhist and Taoist traditions are too strong to remain suppressed for much longer.

India alone as a country has the potential to take the role of spiritually guiding the world. But if there is corruption in India, in its leaders and thinkers, it can have no moral force in the world or even within its own borders. Or if India is unwilling to offend any country, group or religion by challenging the negative and thoughtless practices of our times, it will have no voice.

To compromise with falsehood is not tolerance or nonviolence. It is self-destruction. To turn away in fear or hesitation, not to stand up for what one believes is true, is not modesty but self-betrayal. The world needs a spiritual and moral force that speaks out, or a Divine silence that makes us question all that we do. Not only the leaders of India, whether political, intellectual or religious, must arise with the force of Arjuna, they must defend humanity as a whole, the environment as a whole, the Earth as our Mother, religion as a force of universality and peace. This is not merely to tell everyone that they are right and approve of all cultures and all religions. It is to be the conscience of the world and most people will not like to hear its voice, as we have been ignoring it so much and for so long.

The true leaders and teachers of India—those who are willing to defend at all costs the religion of Truth and the culture of universality—must speak out. And if they do, Vishnu will come again and for the whole world.

However for this to occur India must undergo a radical change. India today does not represent the soul of India but only its shadow. It is inexcusable for the land of the Rishis to be filled with such corruption, ignorance and servility as pervades the country today. Those who know the true spiritual greatness of India can only be shocked and disheartened to see the state of the country. Yet the rest of the world is no better. The Western world has only succeeded in greed, materialism and religious dogma, not in the spiritual life. For this India, with all its shortcomings, still holds the torch, however feeble.

Let India awaken and for this the true spirit of Arjuna must arise! This is the prayer for the next millennium and for the world's deliverance.

1.2 Hinduism in Crisis

A new "quit India movement" has arisen in recent years. Unlike the old quit India movement, which was established by Indian freedom fighters in the early part of the century to remove the British rule from India, the recent movement has an opposite intent—to embrace Western materialist culture and abandon traditional Hindu culture and spirituality perhaps altogether. This movement is very strong in India itself, particularly among so-called modern Hindus, who are largely Western educated and trained to look at their native tradition with alien values and suspicious eyes. The intellectual elite of India takes pride in being in contact with the latest developments in Western culture, art, science and technology, while remaining ignorant and unappreciative of traditional Hindu teachings.

Not all of these Westernized Hindus have actually studied in the West, nor do they need to. The educational system of India itself follows primarily Western standards and values. While the British may have left India physically, their Hindu emulators still run much of the country and see it largely like the British did as a realm to be remade in a Western image. However it is not merely a British model that they follow but a Marxist-Socialist model with its atheistic and anti-nationalistic orientation. The stifling bureaucracy of India, which is finally beginning to break down, is not the product of Hinduism but an imitation of the

Soviet style of administration introduced through Nehru to thwart the development of capitalism.

Part of this quit India movement has expressed itself in a number of Hindus emigrating to other countries, particularly for better job benefits. There are now small but significant Hindu minorities in many Western countries including the United States and Great Britain. Yet Hindus abroad generally appreciate their own traditional culture better than Westernized Hindus residing in India. The reason for this is that Hindus abroad, living apart from their cultural base, have developed a nostalgia for it. They have also seen the limitations of Western culture—its crime, drugs, promiscuity, greed and almost total lack of spiritual values—which is demonstrated to them daily, particularly through the mass media. This makes traditional Hindu values of family, natural living and spirituality more appealing to them, even if they are not possible to accomplish.

Modern Hindus in India see the tremendous social problems of India today, which they tend to blame on the Hindu religion. This is rather strange because India has been ruled by such Westernized Hindus since the partition of India over forty years ago and prior to that had the foreign rule of the British for two hundred years and over five hundred years of Islamic rule by Afghans and Turks before that, who all along have been blaming the Hindu religion for the problems of India under their rule. India has not been under predominantly Hindu rulers for the better part of a millennium. How can such rulers be the cause of the condition of the country today?

However, a new movement is now developing to counter to this Westernization phase. A number of Hindus today are looking to rediscover their Hindu roots, and this has also become a strong movement among Hindu emigrants to foreign countries. This movement is not simply a regressive return to medieval Hindu values, but a rediscovery of the validity and importance of Hindu culture and spirituality for both the future as well as the past. It includes discovering the importance of Hindu Yoga, Vedanta, Ayurveda, Vedic astrology, classical Indian art and culture, and the Hindu view of society and government. A number of Hindus in India are working to make Hinduism more a living presence in the country, with a social and cultural, as well as religious influence. This I would call the "new Hinduism," those who are embracing Hinduism from both a point of tradition and one of modernity, recognizing its real meaning as Sanatana Dharma (the Eternal Tradition) and its relevance for the entire world.

For example, the new Hinduism is bringing back traditional Hindu accounts of history, like the rejection of the Aryan invasion theory, which recent archeological discoveries in India, like the rediscovery of the Sarasvati river, are also proving. They are rejecting the idea that the history of India should be written from a European perspective, as if anything good in India only came from the West (which is the present view). They hold that Hindu values, a culture of Dharma, has its place in the educational system of India, which should not merely imitate Western intellectual or political views, like the Marxist views which have dominated most of the universities of India over the past several decades.

Westernized Hindus generally try to hide their Hindu roots. They do not like to be seen going to temples, though they may go to churches and mosques as a demonstration of their universality in religion. They ignore Hindu social causes like the mistreatment of Hindus in Fiji or in Islamic countries like Bangladesh, Pakistan or Malaysia or the fact that Hindus working in Arab countries are not allowed to practice their religion in public. However, they will take a stand for Palestinian rights in order to show their humanitarianism and global concerns.

Such Westernized Hindus are suspicious of the new Hinduism. They label it out of hand as fundamentalist, backward, or fascist, even though Hinduism is the most liberal, universal, syncretic and diverse of all the world's main religions with its many Gods, sages, scriptures and yogic practices. Westernized Hindus appear to take pride in denigrating Hinduism. On the other hand, they do not criticize religions like Islam or Christianity which are generally exclusive, monolithic, militant and not accepting of other beliefs the way Hinduism is. They like to paint Hinduism as fundamentalist and dangerous while promoting a tolerant and respectful view of Christianity and Islam, including their fundamentalist sides. They have little tolerance for vocal Hindu religious groups like the VHP (Vishwa Hindu Parishad) but they have a great tolerance, for example, for the government of Iran, which Western countries like the United States, have labelled a terrorist country, but which the government of India has been friendly toward, even at one point considering selling nuclear reactors to the country and proclaiming a period of national mourning when Ayatollah Khomeni died.

Contrary to this East to West movement there has been a smaller but still important movement within Western culture itself. Many Westerners have developed an interest in Eastern spirituality including Hindu Yoga, Vedanta, and Ayurveda following a West to East movement. There are now ashrams, temples and Yoga centers throughout the Western world and in much of Asia as well. Gurus from India have often gained large followings in the West. Projecting Hindu spirituality not as backward but as progressive, futuristic and universal in its orientation, they have found it to be appealing to people all over the world. This movement, which began largely in the late sixties, is still increasing on a yearly basis. Now it is moving to Eastern Europe as well, with the collapse of communism. It has even proved at times popular in Islamic countries, but has been suppressed by the authorities there.

Westernized Hindus are naturally perplexed by this movement. It makes them feel perhaps a little guilty that Westerners find value in their spiritual tradition which they have probably never studied or taken seriously. They would like to believe that such Westerners are uneducated, misinformed, or merely some fanatic fringe of progressive Western society and its distrust of any spiritual or yogic practices, which many other Westerners, particularly the religious fundamentalists, would label as cults. However many of the Westerners studying or practicing Hindu based teachings are well educated. They include a number of scientists, artists, doctors and teachers. For example, while modern Hindus look down on Hindu mythology, Joseph Campbell broadcast its value on American Educational Television a few years ago. Instead of showing Hindu mythology as a strange superstition, he showed it as a sophisticated spiritual and psychological science.

I myself have been a product of this West to East movement. I discovered Hindu Yoga and Vedanta teachings at a young age in the late sixties, after having studied Western science, art, philosophy and religion. I found in Hindu teachings a science of spirituality that shows us how to understand ourselves and the vast universe in which we live, not as an external phenomenon but as part of the universal consciousness which transcends time and space. Such spiritual knowledge and realization is almost non-existent in Western religions or in Western intellectual culture, which has not yet understood the deeper layers of consciousness like the Hindu sages. Compared to Hindu yogis and spiritual giants, like Ramana Maharshi or Ramakrishna, the intellectual giants of Western culture, like Einstein or Freud, appear like children in intelligence and in understanding life. Compared to them Western religious leaders like the Pope, who reflect little knowledge of higher states of consciousness, appear like beginners in the spiritual realm.

Later in my life, in my thirties after I had written books on Hindu spirituality, including some published in India, I visited India for the first time and had a number of discussions with modern Westernized Hindus. There I contacted the quit India for the West movement first hand. I was appalled at how little so many Hindus either valued or understood their own tradition. They would equate Hindu spirituality with a superstition on par with caste and untouchability. They were fond of quoting Marx or Shakespeare but would certainly not mention the Bhagavad Gita, which they regarded as regressive. They used materialists and atheists like Freud and Marx to interpret the Vedas, if they studied the Vedas at all. While I was interested in visiting temples and ashrams in India, they wanted to talk about the latest developments in Western technology. While I was a vegetarian, they ate meat. While I admired the sculpture in Hindu temples, they preferred modern Western art. While I liked Indian classical music, they liked Western classical music or even rock and roll, if they were younger in age.

Yet more surprisingly, I discovered that the same Westernized and anti-Hindu attitudes were common in the English language press of India, which often appeared more appropriately the press of a foreign or non-Hindu country than that of a land where over eighty percent of the people are Hindus (the vernacular press is better I might add but still reflects the same trends). The English language press of India appears merely as an Indian version of the Western news media, with the same basic types of news and views, only with a more leftist political orientation. There was little of anything in them of Hindu spirituality or little positive said about Hindu culture.

If we look at the English language press of India, the term Hindu occurs mainly relative to various negative appellations like fundamentalist, chauvinist or even fascist—not merely in regard to small or fringe Hindu groups but relative to some of the largest Hindu religious groups. Even the Western news media would rarely, if ever, apply such terms to a majority religion like Christianity or Islam in their own countries, particularly to the largest groups representing the religions. Meanwhile I saw that non-Hindu groups are seldom so criticized in the Indian press, which would make it appear that Hinduism is the more intolerant than other religions, which any real Hindu knows is not the case at all.

While in India, I also came into contact with the new Hinduism, which I had gained an appreciation for through my own studies. Studying the Vedas in the original Sanskrit I discovered that what the Vedas themselves said was quite different than their modern interpretations by Western and even some Indian scholars. The Vedas were twisted by Western scholars to fit into a Eurocentric view of history that saw no significant indigenous civilization in India. I saw how the earlier Western colonial domination of Asia left its mark in the intellectual realm. I was appalled to learn that these colonialist views of the Vedas were still taught in schools in India today (and even embraced by the anti-colonialist Marxists). I decided to take it upon myself to help correct these wrong views, which I have attempted to do in various books and articles that I have written over the past few years.

When I visited India I met with representatives of the new Hinduism, modern Hindus seeking to rediscover their Hindu spiritual roots. They had a broad view of Hinduism as part of a movement toward a global culture and universal spirituality, Hinduism as Sanatana Dharma. Such individuals were generally highly educated, knew a number of languages, had travelled to many countries, and valued Hinduism from a standpoint of intelligence and modernity, not out of lack of contact with the greater world. To my surprise and chagrin, I found that these were often the same people that the English language press of India would label as fundamentalists. They were called fundamentalists not for any aggressive religious conservatism, but for finding real value in Hinduism and not embracing materialist political values. These people demonstrated an appreciation of religion, spirituality and science, such that I found in no fundamentalist groups in America, or in even the orthodox among Western religions. As

I met these representatives of the new Hinduism before I knew of the social and political polarization of India, I could not be influenced by the negative portrayals of them in the press.

Perhaps the greatest irony of this situation is that Westernized Hindus are looking for a universality, humanitarianism and enlightened attitude about life, such as only exists within their own tradition which they are denigrating without ever having really examined. True enlightened culture does not reside in liberal or leftist politics but in the science of Yoga. There is also no conflict between traditional Hindu or dharmic values and the most enlightened and global values of humanity. One can promote traditional Hindu spiritual values and not only be modern, but super-modern and futuristic, not only Indian but universal. Traditional Hindu spiritual values promote a culture of Dharma, a yogic way of life, a life in harmony with the universe, through recognizing the same Self in all beings.

There is certainly much wrong with India today. Yet it is wrong to think that these problems are simply caused by Hinduism. Certainly they are not caused by Hindu spirituality, which is the most comprehensive, liberal and expansive in the world with its view that all the world is one family and all the universe is One Self. Some of these problems, like the caste system, have their roots in the Hindu social system. But these are usually not based on a real understanding of Hindu cultural forms but on their misapplication through time, in which they have become rigid.

There are indeed some Hindu groups which could be called fanatic, backwards, or superstitious. But these represent only a small part of Hinduism and very few of the Hindu groups which have been accused of these things. Compared to Western religions the percentage of Hindus who have exclusive and intolerant ideas about religion is very small. In fact most so-called fundamentalist Hindus have a far more liberal view of religion than orthodox or even liberal Christians and Muslims.

Many of the problems of modern India have been caused by socialism and communism. In this regard the economic and social problems in India have their parallels in all communist countries today. Many problems in India have their roots in centuries of foreign domination that causes a people to lose their self-respect and cease making efforts to improve themselves. This has been aggravated by the prevalence of anti-Hindu ideological movements, like Communism, Christianity and Islam, which still maintain a strong missionary presence in India.

What the English language news media of India portrays as a battle between modern secular liberals and backward Hindu fundamentalists is more commonly a struggle between a corrupt and rigid communist-socialist elite and traditional Hindu spiritual groups concerned with the real welfare of the country. The so-called militant Hindu fundamentalists are seldom really militant or fundamentalist, but simply a voice of political dissent. The so-called secular liberals include corrupt politicians sustaining themselves by various vote banks through promoting social division along religious and caste lines—the very things they accuse the Hindu groups of doing.

Each country, like each person, has a soul and a destiny. India has her soul and its destiny, which is to be a land of religious freedom and spiritual practices. Unless a person lives up to their soul value or Dharma, he or she cannot be successful or happy in life. The same is true of a country. It is not the soul or Dharma of India to become another Westernized economic giant, which is not to say that India needs to remain poor. It is not her Dharma to become another communist land, and communism is already a thing of the past. Nor is it her Dharma to adapt an exclusive religious belief like that of Islam or Christianity, which claim that other religions are false, inferior or out of date. Above all, it is not India's Dharma to slavishly imitate the West in culture, mind or religion.

India must wake up to her destiny, which is to revive her

spiritual culture and share it for the benefit of all mankind. This requires that the intellectual elite of the country cease denigrating the soul of India in hasty and superficial attempts to be modern and humanitarian. It requires a new Hinduism that corrects the social evils of the older Hinduism while maintaining the greater spiritual basis of the tradition. Such a new Hinduism or awakening to Sanatana Dharma, the Universal Tradition, is essential not only for India but for the entire world. Without reconnecting with our older spiritual traditions and their yogic sciences we will not have the foundation to move forward to a real enlightened age for humanity. Fortunately India appears to be beginning this awakening, however slow, difficult or painful it may be.

1.3
Misrepresentations of Hinduism in the Press

Hindus do not have a history of invading other countries. They have not sent missionaries to other countries preaching to them that their own religions are evil and trying to persuade or intimidate them to adopt Hindu beliefs. They have not economically exploited other countries as their colonies. They have never said that Truth or God belongs only to Hindus and those who believe otherwise are unholy or sinners. Hindus have a history of tolerance and respect for all religions, which is almost unparalleled in the rest of the world. Yet we find that in the news media, including that of India itself, anti-Hindu attitudes are common. Hindus are spoken of in a negative way that is not done relative to religious groups whose behavior has been more violent, exclusive or oppressive. Anti-Hindu statements appear to be acceptable to everyone and no one questions them very much.

Let us take the Ayodhya incident in December of 1992. Newspapers throughout the world stated that "Hindu Militants Destroy Mosque," projecting the image of Hindus both as militants and as mosque destroyers. But what really took place and what is the history behind it?

Hindu groups involved did demolish a building that was built by a Muslim invader from Central Asia some four centuries ago, and the building had been used as a mosque, but not for over fifty years—which was the last time Islamic worship was performed there. In recent years the so-called Ayodhya mosque, Babri Masjid, has only been used for Hindu worship, and it has contained Hindu religious statues in it since 1949. The structure was not originally constructed in the style of a true mosque, lacking minarets and other architecture of a typical mosque. Above all, the site was claimed by the Hindus as the original location of a great Hindu temple to Lord Rama, one of the Hindu Divine incarnations, that was first demolished for the building of the mosque or victory monument by invading Muslim armies. Hindus (and Sikhs we might add) fought dozens of battles over the centuries to reclaim the site and succeeded several times in holding it under their power. The site was not in any Muslim holy place like Mecca or Medina but in one of the seven sacred cities of the Hindus. Calling the site a mosque is thus inaccurate. It should have been called a "disputed structure," which is how newspapers in India generally designate it.

Yet the press did not say that "Hindus destroy a disputed structure in their sacred city of Ayodhya, which Moslems had not used as a mosque for fifty years," because this would not have been much of a story. The result was that the press not only misrepresented what the Hindus had done but inflamed Islamic sentiments, which added fuel to the riots that followed, which were mainly initiated by the Muslim community of India on the belief that one of their sacred sites had been wrongly desecrated by the idolatrous Hindus.

During the Islamic invasions of India—which were not provoked by any Hindu attack on Islamic lands and which lasted for over a thousand years—tens of thousands of Hindu temples were destroyed, in fact most that existed on the subcontinent. The many great temples that Chinese travellers in the seventh century saw throughout India, which were not only Hindu, but Buddhist and Jain, cannot be found today. These temples were not abandoned suddenly, nor did they disappear of their own accord. The invading Muslims willfully destroyed them in an attempt to force Hindus to convert to their faith, or to steal the jewels that Hindu temples abound in. The most sacred temples of the Hindus, like those built on the birthplaces of Rama and Krishna, were special targets. Not only were temples destroyed they were often replaced with mosques, converted into mosques or bricks from demolished temples were used to build mosques. The temple deities were often buried at the entrance of such mosques so that Muslims could trample over them as they entered into their mosques, thus humiliating the Hindus further.

The cruel history of the Islamic invasion of India—which involved massive genocide and enslavement of Hindus—is not known by many people, particularly in the West where the history of Asia is not regarded as very important. Some would like to pretend that it didn't exist at all, or that the scale of atrocities was really very small, that its intentions were not religious conversion but military conquest, or that being a thing of the past we ought to forget about it today in order to protect communal harmony in the country.

India partitioned itself in 1947 in favor of the Muslim minority, which claimed that it could not live in a Hindu majority state. In the process the Hindu temples left in Pakistan were taken over by the Muslims and frequently destroyed. Even the governments and armies of Pakistan and Bangladesh at times have participated in such Hindu temple destruction activity. The real history of India is thus one of Hindu temples being routinely destroyed by Muslims on a massive scale, and yet this is seldom recounted. In the Ayodhya incident this history was conveniently ignored. On the contrary, the image of Hindus as mosque-destroyers was portrayed, not that of Muslims as temple-destroyers which is a much more accurate depiction.

At the same time as the Ayodhya demolition, and in retaliation for it, dozens of Hindu temples were destroyed in Pakistan and Bangladesh. Some were attacked in Great Britain and other countries outside of India as well. Yet such stories were treated as mere footnotes to the Ayodhya mosque destruction, as if the Hindus were responsible for them by what they did with one disputed mosque, and Muslims were not responsible for their own actions once provoked by Hindus.

If we look at how the news media treated the event it appears that one Hindu demolition of a disputed mosque is more newsworthy and an expression of greater intolerance than Islamic destruction of any number of Hindu temples. Is this not prejudice and an anti-Hindu attitude of great proportions? Why is the destruction of Hindu temples not a newsworthy item, but the destruction of one disputed mosque worth global headlines? In fact Muslims also destroy the mosques of other Muslim sects, like the Ahmadiya mosques which have been destroyed in Pakistan, and this is not treated as a newsworthy item either.

The real question that should have been asked after the Ayodhya incident was why did Hindus finally take to this demolition, when for over a thousand years they have allowed their temples to be routinely destroyed and turned into mosques with little retaliation? The question itself provides the answer. Whether one approves of the act or not, such a history can create a sense of injustice for which revindication may be sought, particularly if it is not addressed through legal means. The news media also failed to give importance to the fact that the Ayodhya dispute had been in the courts of India for over forty years, with no decision as to whether the structure was really a mosque or a temple that had been stolen.

Hindus, like many other oppressed peoples, appear to be waking up to the history of their oppression. Like other racial, religious or sexual oppressed groups, this awakening involves a release of anger or hostility which can appear extreme and is certainly contrary to what has been their normal behavior. Yet it can hardly be simply condemned as the news media appears to be attempting. It is part of a process of rectification that will eventually find its balance. Given the modern age of information, wherein the facts of history are known, and wherein oppressed groups of all types are awakening and seeking to gain equality, we must expect that Hindus will also go through this process. Westerners may not be accustomed to regarding Hindus as an oppressed group, but if we examine the history of India we see that Hindus have been subject to racial and religious oppression, along with economic and military aggression since the Muslim invasions of the eighth century, followed by the actions of the Portuguese and the British in the colonial era. So far modern India has not yet adequately dealt with its past.

What should really interest us is not why Hindus took to this demolition but how Hindus could tolerate the massive destruction of their temples for centuries with such forbearance. This is an act of tolerance unprecedented in Western history. That it should now appear to be coming to an end should not shock anyone. The real wonder is that it lasted for so long. The issue should get us to look at the historical grievances of the Hindus, which they are certainly entitled to claim. Even if one regards the Ayodhya demolition as wrong, it is hard not to feel some sympathy with Hindu historical grievances on these issues once the matter has been studied thoroughly.

To examine the issue of anti-Hindu attitudes in the press further, let us compare how India is treated with how two other countries are treated. The first is Saudi Arabia in which all religions are illegal except for Islam. Other religious practices are not allowed except in private and for foreigners only. There is no difference between church, state and police, which is all run according to traditional Islamic law. By all accounts Saudi Arabia is an intolerant fundamentalist state. It has funded various Islamic fundamentalist and terrorist groups all over the world through the years. However Saudi Arabia is called a "moderate" Islamic country. If Hindus were to try to do in India, even a small portion of what the Saudis have done in their country, the world community would be appalled and might even take up arms against them.

Why is Saudi Arabia treated specially? The answer is very simple, because of world dependency on Saudi oil. Economic need fashions the global press and structures global ethics. We can ignore the intolerance of those whom we want to have good business relations with. Since the Western world, which dominates the mass media, has little economic need for India, India is treated unfairly in the press (though with the economic liberalization of India and more interest in India economically by the West this may change in time). There is no need economically to cater to the Hindus, and no threat of Hindu retaliation economically or through terrorism, so they can be unfairly condemned or bullied.

Next let us compare how India is treated relative to that of China, a communist dictatorship, whereas India is a democracy. China has long held the most favored nation trading status with the United States, in spite of the Tienanmen massacre in Peking a few years ago. Anti-Chinese attitudes are seldom found in the press. Chinese are seldom criticized for militancy—and no real action is taken against them—even though they sell weapons of mass destruction and nuclear technology to other countries and have had an ongoing campaign of genocide of the people of Tibet. Why is China treated differently than India? It appears also to be potential economic gain, as well as fear of China's size and power. It is curious to note how humanitarian issues follow economic imperatives and that countries which are economically valuable can be easily excused for their violations of human rights, while countries that have little economic importance can be either ignored or denigrated.

Next, let us compare how the Hindu minority is treated in Islamic countries with the treatment of the Islamic minority in India. Pakistan eliminated its Hindu minority long ago through forceful conversion or genocide. There are almost no Hindus left in a land which before partition had a significant minority of them. Yet hardly anyone even cares to mention this fact. The Hindu minority in Bangladesh has been continually oppressed and dispossessed of its property, and is therefore dwindling in number. Yet the global press does not mention this either. While it has been recognized that the genocide in Bangladesh in 1971-72 was one of the worst in history and numbered over three million people, the press seldom mentions the fact that it was mainly Hindus who were killed. Hindus who work in Arabic countries are not allowed to practice their religion in public and yet no country, including India, protests this, though non-Hindus working in India are certainly not prevented from public worship (and would certainly protest fiercely if this were attempted).

On the other hand, though Muslims may be subject to some degree of discrimination in India and are certainly very poor, their numbers have grown, and many Muslim immigrants have come to India from Bangladesh, several million. Clearly India has not stifled Islam the way Pakistan and Bangladesh have stifled Hinduism. India has allowed Islam to increase within its borders, while Pakistan has all but eliminated Hinduism from its. Moreover India has more Islamic sects than any Islamic country, with some, like the Ahmadiyas who have been made illegal in Pakistan, taking their refuge in non-Islamic India! Yet the Ayodhya incident proclaims Hindu mistreatment of Muslims and does not mention the much greater Muslim mistreatment of Hindus. It appears that Hindu mistreatment of Muslims is a newsworthy item, while Muslim mistreatment of Hindus, even on a much larger scale, is not.

In countries like Pakistan or Bangladesh Hindu temples can be destroyed or taken over easily. They have no government protection like mosques in India. Hence it is not an issue if temples are destroyed in the normal course of things, and cannot possibly provoke any national crisis, as is the case in India.

Why is there such a disparity of treatment? The greater number of Islamic countries and the influence of petrodollars is certainly part of this, as is the fear of Islamic terrorist retaliation. India's own lack of concern for Hindus in other countries is another factor. This often goes back to leftist and Marxist influences in India who are opposed to the Hindu religion which is their main political opposition in the country.

The Western press also proclaims Hinduism as polytheism and idolatry, not as monism and spirituality, which it really is. Hindu practices of Yoga and meditation, its seeking of cosmic consciousness and view of Self-realization as the highest goal of life, and its many great modern sages like Ramakrishna, Aurobindo, and Ramana Maharshi are seldom given any credit. The sophisticated nature of Hindu philosophy, psychology and cosmology are generally ignored. Western news media accounts of India generally focus on such social evils as the caste system, mistreatment of women and dowry deaths, without showing the deeper side of Hinduism. This would be like representing American culture through drug addiction, sexual promiscuity and divorce courts and ignoring the other aspects of the culture.

Or if the spiritual teachings of India are mentioned, they are regarded as "cults," even though they have been the fabric of one of the greatest civilizations of the world through history. It appears that any religious teaching not part of traditional Western culture is liable to be called a cult in the Western press, particularly if it gains any following. How would Western people feel if predominant Western religions were called cults in the Eastern world? How would Christians feel if the news media of India called Christianity a cult? Christian missionaries in India have broken up families and sowed dissension in Hindu society far more effectively than any so-called Hindu cult leaders in the West. The Waco Texas incident in 1993, in which ninety followers of Christian cult leader David Koresh were killed, has been used to attack Hindu and other Eastern religious groups in America as cults, in spite of the fact that Koresh, like Jim Jones, the other recent cult leader who led great numbers of his followers to death, was a Christian!

Some Hindus themselves claim that Hindus must be subject to a higher standard, that their religion does not allow the violence or intolerance that other religions may accept or even promote. Hence oppression of Hindus does not bother them as much as Hindus oppressing non-Hindus. Yet to create a higher standard for Hindus does not mean to misrepresent their behavior relative to other groups. We cannot say that temple destroying is alright for Muslims because it is part of their religion, but reclaiming mosques built on Hindu sacred sites is not right for Hindus who should follow a policy of total religious tolerance. There must be one standard for all human beings. The higher standard of tolerance in the Hindu religion does not mean that anything that suggests intolerance among Hindus should be broadcast to the global media as a great evil, while intolerant actions among other groups, particularly against Hindus, should be ignored.

There should be a common standard for all humanity and Hindu groups should not be especially attacked, while other groups are ignored or excused for what may be more violent or intolerant behavior. Hindus need not be given any special favorable treatment, but the special unfavorable treatment of them which now exists should come to an end. Hindus should be portrayed not just for what the Western mind finds wrong with them but as they are. The full extent of Hindu culture, religion and spirituality should be made known.

Given all this, it is imperative that anti-Hindu attitudes are questioned. They are a form of ethnic and religious discrimination, which should be unacceptable to any open minded person. As long as such negative attitudes persist in the press they can only further misunderstanding and disharmony. Yet the place where they must be changed first is in the English language press of India. We cannot expect the global press not to follow anti-Hindu attitudes that come from India itself. And India can never rise up as long as it is attacking itself.

This does not mean that the freedom of the press in India or elsewhere should be challenged or curtailed. Freedom is essential in the dissemination of information and no religion should have control over that. It means that Hindus should cease being passive relative to their own news media and enter into a dialogue with it, including questioning or criticizing it when it misrepresents their traditions. If media groups do not respond to such criticism Hindus should cease supporting them or create their own alternative media which more accurately represents their views. Ultimately if Hindus fail to represent their views adequately, particularly in India, they have no one to blame but themselves.

As a Westerner who has studied the deeper side of Hinduism and learned how much Hinduism is misrepresented and misunderstood, I have been compelled to speak out on these issues. Greater communication on these issues would probably go far in correcting this anti-Hindu prejudice. Given the extent of the problem it will take time to correct and the vested interests who are opposed to it will not give in easily. However there are now those who are presenting the Truth and the old distortions will no longer go unchallenged.

In closing, I am not saying that Hindus have not done anything wrong or that there is nothing questionable about Hindu political groups or social practices. Hindus must take it upon themselves to reform their society, which is badly needed, but this should be done according to the soul of India, which is Dharma, not according to Western political, intellectual or religious ideologies, which are generally adharmic, that is unspiritual, however modern or well-funded they may be.

1.4
Hindu Fundamentalism: What is It?

Fundamentalism is an easily discernible phenomenon in belief-oriented religions like Christianity and Islam which have a simple and exclusive pattern to their faith. They generally insist that there is only One God, who has only one Son or final Prophet, and only one true scripture, which is literally God's Word. They hold that belief in this One God and his chief representative brings salvation in an eternal heaven and disbelief causes condemnation to an eternal hell. Muslims daily chant "there is no God but Allah and Mohammed is his (last) prophet." Most Christians, whether Catholic or Protestant, regard belief in Christ as one's personal savior as the only true way to salvation.

Fundamentalists are literalists in these traditions who hold rigidly to their beliefs and insist that since their religion alone is true the other religions should not be tolerated, particularly in the lands where members of their religion are in a majority. Fundamentalists generally hold to their religion's older social customs and refuse to integrate into the broader stream of modern society which recognizes freedom of religious belief.

Fundamentalism can usually be discriminated from orthodoxy in these traditions, but tends to overlap with it, particularly in the case of Islam. Most orthodox Christians and many orthodox Muslims tolerate those of other religious beliefs, though they may not agree with them, and are not involved in the militancy and social backwardness of fundamentalist groups. They usually have little trouble functioning in modern society, though they may keep to themselves in matters of religion and still regard that their's is the only true religion. The strictly orthodox in these religions, however, may not be very different than the fundamentalists and often support them.

While the news media of the Western World, and of India itself, speaks of Hindu fundamentalism, no one appears to have really defined what it is. Is there a Hindu fundamentalism comparable to Islamic or Christian fundamentalism? Using such a term merely assumes that there is, but what is the evidence for it? Are there Hindu beliefs of the same order as the absolute beliefs of fundamentalist Christianity and Islam? It is questionable that, whatever problems might exist in Hinduism, whether fundamentalism like that found in Christianity or Islam can exist at all in its more open and diverse tradition which has many names and forms for God, many great teachers and Divine incarnations, many sacred books, and a pursuit of Self-realization that does not recognize the existence of any eternal heaven or hell. There is no monolithic faith called Hinduism with a set system of beliefs that all Hindus must follow which can be turned into such fundamentalism.

Fundamentalist groups insist that their's is the only true God and that all other Gods or names for God are wrong. Islamic fundamentalists insist that the only God is Allah, and will not accept Hindu names like Brahman or Ishvara, even though these also refer to a Supreme Being and Ultimate Spiritual Reality such as Allah is supposed to be. Christian fundamentalists will not accept Allah or Brahman as names for God as they conceive Him to be. Hindus with their many names and forms for God don't mind accepting the Christian name God or even Islamic Allah as referring to the same reality, though they may not use these names in the same strict or exclusive sense as Christians or Muslims. A belief in God is not even necessary to be a Hindu, as such non-theistic Hindu systems as Sankhya reveal. For those who speak of Hindu fundamentalism, we must ask the question: What One God do Hindu fundamentalist groups insist upon is the only true God and which Gods are they claiming are false except for Him? If Hindus are not insisting upon the sole reality of the One Hindu God can they be called fundamentalists like the Christians and Muslims?

Islamic fundamentalists consider that Islam is the only true religion, that no true new faith can be established after Islam and that with the advent of Islam all previous faiths, even if they were valid up to that time, became outdated. Christian fundamentalists hold that Christianity alone is true, and that Islam and Hinduism are religions of the devil. Even orthodox people in these traditions may hold these views.

Hindus are not of one faith only. They are divided into Shaivites (those who worship Shiva), Vaishnavas (those who worship Vishnu), Shaktas (those who worship the Goddess), Ganapatas (those who worship Ganesh), Smartas and a number of other groups which are constantly being revised relative to modern teachers around whom new movements may be founded (like the Swami Narayan movement, the Ramakrishna-Vivekananda groups or the followers of Sri Aurobindo). Those called Hindu fundamentalists are similarly divided up into these different sects. What common belief can be found in all these groups which constitutes Hindu fundamentalism? What common Hindu fundamentalist platform do the different sects of Hinduism share? Is it a Shaivite, Vaishnava or other type fundamentalism? How do such diverse groups maintain their harmony and identity under the Hindu fundamentalist banner? While one can make a code of belief for Christian or Islamic fundamentalism, what code of belief applies to Hindu fundamentalism of all different sects?

No Hindus—including so-called Hindu fundamentalists—insist that there is only one true faith called Hinduism and that all other faiths are false. Hinduism contains too much plurality to allow for that. Its tendency is not to coalesce into a fanatic unity like the fundamentalists of other religions, but to disperse into various diverse sects and fail to arrive at any common action, historically even one of self-defense against foreign invaders.

Fundamentalist groups insist upon belief in the literal truth of one book as the Word of God, which they base their behavior on. Muslim fundamentalists insist that the Koran is the Word of God and that all necessary knowledge is contained in it. Christian fundamentalists say the same thing of the Bible. Again even orthodox or ordinary Muslims and Christians often believe this. Hindus have many holy books like the Vedas, Agamas, Bhagavad Gita, Ramayana and so on, which contain a great variety of teachings and many different points of view and no one of these books is required reading for all Hindus. Hindus generally respect the holy books of other religions as well. What single holy book do Hindu fundamentalists hold literally to be the word of God, which they base their behavior upon? Christian and Islamic fundamentalists flaunt their holy book and are ever quoting from it to justify their actions. What Hindu Bible are the Hindu fundamentalists all carrying, quoting and preaching from and finding justification in?

Fundamentalist groups are often involved in conversion activity to get other people to adopt their beliefs. They frequently promote missionary efforts throughout the world to bring the entire world to their views. This again is true of ordinary or orthodox Muslims and Christians. Fundamentalists are merely more vehement in their practices. What missionary activities are Hindu fundamentalists promoting throughout the world? What missions in other countries have Hindu fundamentalists set up to convert Christians, Muslims or those of other beliefs to the only true religion called Hinduism? What Hindus are motivated by a missionary spirit to discredit people of other religious beliefs in order to convert and save them?

Fundamentalist groups not only condemn those of other

beliefs to an eternal hell, they may even make death threats against those who criticize their beliefs. The fatwa of the Ayatollah Khomeni against Salman Rushdie and of some others against Anwar Shaikh (a name not so well known but not untypical) are examples of this, which many Muslim groups throughout the world, perhaps the majority, have accepted. What Hindu has ever condemned non-Hindus to an eternal hell, or issued declarations asking for the death of anyone for merely criticizing Hindu beliefs? Where have Hindus ever stated that it is punishable by death to criticize Krishna, Rama or any other great Hindu leader? There are certainly plenty of books, including many by Christians and Muslims, which portray Hinduism in a negative light. How many of such books are Hindu fundamentalists trying to ban, and how many of their authors are they threatening?

Fundamentalists are usually seeking to return to the social order and customs of some ideal religious era of a previous age. Fundamentalists often insist upon returning to some traditional law code like the Islamic Sharia or Biblical law codes, which are often regressive by modern standards of justice and humanitarianism. What law code are Hindu fundamentalists seeking to reestablish? Which Hindu groups are agitating for the return of the law code of the Manu Samhita, for example (which incidentally has a far more liberal and spiritual law code than the Sharia or the Bible)?

Fundamentalists are usually opposed to modern science. Many Christian and Islamic fundamentalists reject the theory of evolution and insist that the world was created by God some 6000 years ago. Even in America Christian fundamentalists are trying to have this theory taught in the public schools and would like to have the evolution theory taken out. What scientific theories are Hindu fundamentalists opposed to and trying to prevent being taught in schools today?

Fundamentalism creates various political parties limited to

members of that religion only, which aim at setting up religious dictatorships. What exclusively Hindu religious party exists in India or elsewhere in the world, and what is its common Hindu fundamentalist platform? Who is asking for a Hindu state that forbids the practice of other religions, allows only Hindu religious centers to be built and requires a Hindu religious figure as the head of the country?. This is what other fundamentalist groups are asking for in terms of their religions and what they have instituted in a number of countries that they have taken power, like Iran and Saudi Arabia.

Fundamentalism is often involved with militancy and sometimes with terrorism. What Hindu minorities in the world are violently agitating for their separate state? What planes have Hindu fundamentalists hijacked, what hostages have they taken, what bombs have they planted? What terrorist activities are Hindu fundamentalists promoting throughout the world? What countries are stalking down Hindu fundamentalist terrorists who are plotting against them? The Ayatollah Khomeni is regarded in the Western world as a typical example of an Islamic fundamentalist militant leader. Many Western people consider him to be a terrorist as well. What Hindu fundamentalist leader has a similar record?

Saudi Arabia is usually regarded as a pious or orthodox Islamic country, and is usually not called fundamentalist even by the news media of India. No non-Islamic places of worship are allowed to be built there. No non-Islamic worship is allowed in public. American troops in the Gulf War had to hide their religious practices so as not to offend the Saudis. Traditional Islamic law, including mutilation for various offences, is strictly enforced by a special religious police force. If we apply any standard definition of fundamentalism, Saudi Arabia is a super-fundamentalist country. What Hindu community is insisting upon the same domination of one religious belief, law and social practices like that of Saudi Arabia? Which Hindus are more fundamentalist in their beliefs and practices than the Saudis, whom few are calling fundamentalists?

Hence we must ask: What are Hindus being accused as fundamentalists for doing? Is it belief in the unique superiority of their religion, the sole claim of their scripture as the Word of God, their savior or prophet as ultimate for all humanity, that those who believe in their religion go to an eternal heaven and those who don't go to an eternal hell, the need to convert the world to their beliefs? These views are found not only in Christian and Islamic fundamentalism but even among the orthodox. There are no Hindu fundamentalist statements of such nature. Can we imagine any Hindu swearing that there is no God but Rama and Tulsidas is his only prophet, that the Ramayana is the only true scripture, that those who believe differently will be condemned by Rama to eternal damnation and those who criticize Tulsidas should be killed?

Hindus are called fundamentalists for wanting to retake a few of their old holy places, like Ayodhya, of the many thousands destroyed during centuries of foreign domination. Several Hindu groups are united around this cause. This, however, is an issue oriented movement, not the manifestation of a monolithic fundamentalism. It is a unification of diverse groups to achieve a common end, not the product of a uniform belief system. Even the different groups involved have often been divided as to how to proceed and have not spoken with any single voice. Whether one considers the action to be right or wrong, it is not the manifestation of fundamentalism. It may be the awakening of a number of Hindus socially and politically but it is not the assertion of any single or exclusive religious ideology. If it is fundamentalism, what is the fundamentalist ideology, belief and practice behind it? Hindus, alone of all people, have failed to take back their holy sites after the end of the colonial era. If they are fundamentalists for seeking to do so, then what should we call Pakistan or Bangladesh, who have destroyed many Hindu holy sites and were not simply taking back Islamic sites that the Hindus had previously usurped?

Hindus are called fundamentalists for organizing themselves politically. Yet members of all other religions have done this, *while Hinduism is by all accounts the most disorganized of all religions*. There are many Christian and Islamic parties throughout the world, and in all countries where these religions are in a majority they make sure to exert whatever political influence they can. Why shouldn't Hindus have a political voice even in India? The Muslims in India have their own Muslim party and no one is calling them fundamentalists for organizing themselves politically. There are many Islamic states throughout the world and in these Hindus, if they exist at all, are oppressed. What Hindu groups are asking for India to be a more strictly Hindu state than Muslims are doing in Islamic states?

There are those who warn that Hindu rule would mean the creation of a Hindu theocratic state? Yet what standard Hindu theology is there, and what Hindu theocratic state has ever existed? Will it be a Shaivite, Vaishnava, or Vedantic theocracy? What Hindu theocratic model will it be based upon? Is there a model of Hindu kings like the Caliphs of early Islam to go back to, or like the Christian emperors of the Middle Ages? What famous Hindu king was a fundamentalist who tried to eliminate all other beliefs from the land or tried to spread Hinduism throughout the world by the sword? Does Rama or Krishna provide such a model? Does Shivaji provide such a model? If no such model exists what is the fear of a militant Hindu theocratic rule based upon?

Traditional Hindus do exist. There are Hindus who are caught in conservative or regressive social customs, like untouchability or mistreatment of women, which should not be underestimated. There are serious problems in Hindu society that must be addressed, but these should be examined as per their nature and cause, which is not some uniform Hindu fundamentalism but wrong practices that are often contrary to real Hindu thought. To lump them together as problems of Hindu fundamentalism fails to examine them adequately but, rather, uses them as a scare tactic to discredit Hinduism as a whole. There are some Hindus who may believe that their religion is superior and want to keep it separate from other religions. In this regard they are no different than orthodox Christians and Muslims.

The fact is that there is no monolithic fundamentalism possible among Hindus who have no uniform belief structure. A charge of social backwardness and discriminatory attitudes can be made against a number of Hindus but this is not the same as the blanket charge of fundamentalism, which misinterprets Hinduism as a religion of militancy which it nowhere is. The charge of fundamentalism is usually made against various Hindu groups like the VHP (Vishwa Hindu Parishad), who do not support the caste system and other such backward customs anyway.

What is called Hindu fundamentalism is in fact generally a reaction to Islamic, Christian and Communist fundamentalisms, which are all organized according to an exclusive belief system and a strategy to take over the world. These three fundamentalisms are attacking India from within, as well as threatening it from without. Islamic terrorist activity continues in India, particularly in Kashmir. India is now surrounded by self-proclaimed Islamic states where Hindus have become second class citizens. Under this circumstance why should it be so wrong for Hindus in India to consider creating a state that defends them? What other country is willing to defend the rights or traditions of Hindus? Christian and Islamic missionary activity continues strongly in many parts of India. Do these missionary groups portray Hinduism as a valid religion in its own right? They are sometimes not even teaching respect for India as a nation as the separatist agitation they create once their members become a majority in a region reveals.

Hinduism is a supertolerant religion. No other religion in the world accepts such a diversity of beliefs and practices or is so ready to acknowledge the validity of other religions. The idea of the unity of all religions was practically invented by modern Hindus like Ramakrishna, Vivekananda and Gandhi. As Hinduism is a supertolerant religion, even a little intolerance among Hindus is regarded as Hindu fundamentalism. And the charge of intolerance can be used to discredit Hindu groups, who are extremely sensitive to such a negative portrayal.

Throughout history Islam and Christianity, owing to the exclusive nature of their beliefs, have been generally intolerant religions (though there have been notable exceptions). They have not accepted the validity of other religious practices, and contain in themselves little diversity as compared to Hinduism. What Christian or Muslim leaders proclaim that all religions are one or that Hindus and Buddhists have as valid a religion as they do (and therefore do not need to be converted)? As these religions are generally intolerant, their members have to be superintolerant to be called fundamentalist.

Hindus often have a double standard in religion that works against them. They try to tolerate, accept or even appreciate exclusivism, intolerance and fundamentalism when practiced by those of other religious beliefs. For example, which Hindus are criticizing the far more obvious fundamentalism and exclusivism among Christians and Muslims? Meanwhile any criticism by Hindus of other religions, even when justified, may be regarded by other Hindus as intolerance. In addition, many Hindus, particularly of the modern socialist-communist variety, brand even pride in Hinduism as fundamentalism.

Another related term that we meet with in the Indian press today is that of "Hindu chauvinism," though terms such as "Christian chauvinism" or "Islamic chauvinism" do not occur in either the Indian or the Western press. Chauvinists believe in the special superiority of their particular group. This term is used mainly relative to white chauvinists, those who think that whites are genetically better than dark-skinned people, or in the case of male chauvinists or those who think that men are inherently better than women. Hindus may praise their religion, and Hindus often use flowery and exaggerated language to praise things, but few if any Hindus are claiming that Hindus own the truth and that those of other backgrounds or beliefs cannot find it. Christians and Muslims routinely believe that only members of their religion go to heaven and everyone else, particularly idol worshipping people like Hindus, go to hell. Which Hindu chauvinists have similar ideas? The Vatican recently told its monks and nuns not to experiment with Yoga and Eastern forms of religious practice, which it branded as selfish, false and misleading. Should we not therefore call the Pope a Christian chauvinist religious leader? Yet Hindus who are more tolerant than this may be designated in such a manner.

Hindus are not only not chauvinistic they are generally suffering from a lack of self-esteem and an inferiority complex by which they are afraid to really express themselves or their religion. They have been beaten down by centuries of foreign rule and ongoing attempts to convert them. The British treated them as racially inferior and both Christians and Muslims treated them as religiously perverted. That some Hindus may express pride in their religion is a good sign and shows a Hindu awakening. Unfortunately the groups who may be challenged by this awakening have labelled this pride chauvinistic. Naturally some Hindu groups may express this pride in an excessive way, just as happened with the Black pride idea in America during the civil rights movement, but this is only an attempt to counter a lack of pride and self-respect, it is hardly the assertion of any enduring cultural militancy and does not have the history like the fundamentalism of Christianity and Islam, which goes back to the early eras of these faiths.

Such terms as "fundamentalist" and "chauvinist" are much less applicable to Hinduism than to other religions and generally a great exaggeration. They are a form of name calling, and do not represent any clearly thought out understanding. It is also interesting to note that many of the people who brand Hindus in this light are often themselves members of more exclusivist ideologies, which have an agenda to gain world-domination and to take over India.

This does not mean that Hindus should not be criticized. Certainly they can be criticized for many things. They have to really look at who they are and what they are doing because in most cases they are not living up to their inner potential or their heritage. On a social level many Hindus are trapped in backward social customs, but those who are not backward are usually caught in the corruption or materialism of modern society. On an inner level Hindus suffer from lack of creativity, initiative, and original thinking. They want to imitate either their own older thinkers, whose teachings may not be entirely relevant today, or, if modern, they imitate the trends of Western culture which are unspiritual. As a group Hindus mainly suffer from passivity, disunity, and a lack of organization, and they are very poor at communicating who they are to the world as a whole. Relative to their own religion their main problem is that they fail to study, practice or support it, or to defend it if Hindu teachings are misrepresented or if Hindus are oppressed.

These are not the problems of an aggressive or militant fundamentalism but the opposite, that of people who lack faith and dedication to themselves and their traditions. Hindus are not in danger of being overly active and militant but of remaining so passive, resigned, and apologetic that they are unable to function as a coherent group or speak with a common voice about any issue. They have been very slow even to defend themselves against unwarranted attack, much less to assert themselves or attack others. There is no danger of a monolithic or dictatorial fundamentalism in India, like in Iran or Saudi Arabia. The danger is of a divided and passive religion that leaves itself prey to external forces and thereby gradually disintegrates. A little more activity among Hindus, almost whatever it might be, would be a good sign as it shows that they are not entirely asleep! To brand such activity, which is bound to be agitated at first, as fundamentalist because it causes this sleep to be questioned is a mistake.

In this regard Sri Aurobindo's insight may be helpful (*Indian's Rebirth*, p. 177). He said, "The Christians brought darkness rather than light. That has always been the case with aggressive religions—they tend to overrun the Earth. Hinduism on the other hand is passive, and therein lies its danger."

It is time Hindus stopped accepting wrong designations and negative stereotypes of their wonderful religion. Certain aspects of Hinduism need to be reformed, and Hindus are not all required to agree with each other or accept any set religious dogma, but there is very little in this beautiful religion that warrants such debasing terms as fundamentalism and chauvinism. If we look at the aspects which are commonly ascribed to religious fundamentalism we find little of them even among so-called Hindu fundamentalists.

Hindus who accuse other Hindus of being fundamentalists should really question what they are saying. What is the fundamentalism they see, or is it merely a reaction to the oppression that Hindus have passively suffered for so long? Are the people making the charge of fundamentalism themselves following any religious or spiritual path, or is it a political statement of non-religious people against religion? *If Hindus are becoming intolerant and narrow-minded they should be criticized for being poor Hindus, not for being fundamentalist Hindus,* as true Hinduism has a universal spirit.

As long as Hinduism is devalued and misrepresented we must expect some Hindus to take a stand against this in one way or another. Other Hindus should not simply criticize them if the stand they take may be one-sided. Hindus must try to defend Hinduism in a real way, not simply condemn those who may not be defending it in a way that they think is not correct. This requires projecting a positive Hindu spirit, the yogic spirit, that can attract all Hindus and turn their support of the tradition in a spiritual direction. It requires not condemning other Hindus who are struggling to uphold the tradition as they understand it to be, but arousing them to the true spirit of the religion.

To routinely raise such negative stereotypes as fundamentalist or even fascist relative to Hindu groups, who may only be trying to bring some sense of unity or common cause among Hindus, is a gross abuse of language. What Hindus need is to wake up and unite, to recognize their common spiritual heritage and work together to manifest it in the world today, just as modern teachers like Vivekananda and Aurobindo encouraged. Such teachers did not speak of Hindu fundamentalism. They recognized Hindu backwardness but sought to remedy it by going to the core of Hindu spirituality, the spirit of unity in recognition of the Divine in all, not by trying to cast a shadow on Hinduism as a whole.

1.5
Leftist Scholarship in India

How would you expect that Hinduism, the world's oldest and most complex religion, would appear as seen through the eyes of Marxists? Naturally it would not look very good. After all Karl Marx himself declared that religion was the opiate of the masses. However now communism has fallen all over the world and religion, including Hinduism, is still going strong. We have learned that the real truth has been that Marxism was the opiate of the intellectuals, as it has been called, not that religion itself is an illusion.

Unfortunately, the universities of India have been strongly influenced by Marxists since independence and their view of Hinduism has often become entrenched in the educational system. A name which comes to mind readily is that of Romila Thapar, Emeritus Professor of History at Jawaharlal Nehru University (JNU), which is itself well known in India as a center of Marxist activity. Thapar is neither the most important, nor the most prominent figure of Marxist circles, but she has been very much in the news lately and represents a wider phenomenon, and her name has been picked here for no other reason. She and her colleagues are responsible for a number of textbooks in India on the history of the country, which not surprisingly are negative about the majority religion of the land. Thapar is not unique in her thought, but she affords us a good example of how leftist scholarship has worked in India.

If we understand that historians like Thapar are Marxists the logic behind her studies becomes obvious. Thapar's historical criticisms of Hinduism are quite negative, and it is often easier to get more sympathetic accounts of Hinduism from professors in the West, particularly those who have practiced some Hindu-based yogic or meditational teachings. Thapar even doubts whether Hinduism as a religion really existed until recent times. She portrays Hinduism not as a comprehensive tradition going back to the Mahabharata or to the Vedas, but as a relatively modern appropriation, and therefore misinterpretation, of older practices and symbols, whose real meaning we can no longer know as we are not products of that cultural milieu which produced them in the first place. This view is called "deconstructionism" in the West and is the product of French Marxist thinkers.

By this view Thapar sees Hinduism, and religion in general, as reinterpreting cultural symbols for purposes of social and political exploitation. She tries to point out that Hinduism is mainly a vehicle of social oppression through the caste system and is not worthy of much respect for any modern rational or humanistic person. This is standard deconstructionist thinking about religion which is based on the assumption that there is nothing eternal in human beings and therefore there can be no continuous meaning in religion. In other words she interprets Hinduism and religion, which are supposed to deal with the eternal, only in terms of time and history. Such people have failed to understand the correct development of reason (*buddhi*) according to Hindu sages, whose real purpose is to allow us to discern the transient from the eternal, not to deny the eternal in favor of the transient such as is the movement of the logic of thinkers like Thapar.

In particular, Thapar tries to show that the non-violence and tolerance generally ascribed to Hinduism are myths that Hindus or India never really followed. There are a few historical instances of Hindus being violent or oppressive of Buddhists and

Jains, which she emphasizes. There are also historical instances of Buddhists being oppressive of non-Buddhists. Such is the egoism inherent in human nature that is difficult to root out. But these are exceptions. There is no Hindu or Buddhist tradition of crusades or holy wars like that of Western religions of Christianity and Islam. There is a tradition of non-violence (*ahiṁsā*), which however imperfectly followed, was honored in India more so than anywhere else in the world.

What is most interesting about Thapar's studies of Hinduism is that they are devoid of any spiritual dimension. She ignores the great Hindu yogis and gurus and does not discuss the Hindu philosophy of the universe or higher states of consciousness, which she does not give any validity to. She sees the institution of Sannyasa or monastic renunciation as another source of social authority (and therefore oppression of the masses), not a spiritual institution. Her interpretation of Hinduism follows purely social and political lines. Yet as an atheist and Marxist can we expect that she would understand or appreciate Hindu devotional or yogic practices? You will certainly never find her quoting the Upanishads or the Gita in a favorable light. In this regard I am reminded of a communist poet of Maharashtra whom I once met, who described the Gita as "the greatest mystification the human mind has ever produced." No doubt Thapar would be inclined to concur.

To put together Hinduism and Buddhism along with Christianity and Islam is itself not a very bright idea and can barely be sustained intellectually, but Indian Marxists' view of Hinduism is on the same order as Karl Marx's view of Christianity, or the Chinese communist view of Buddhism. Going to them to understand Hinduism is a lot like going to Marx to understand Christianity or Mao to understand Chinese Buddhism. Following their Marxist mentors, they accuse Hinduism of having a political agenda in the guise of religion (which since there is no God in their view, religion could never have any real spiritual agenda anyway). Yet there is no doubt that such Marxist thinkers, seeing the world only in political terms, have an entirely political agenda. For instance, Thapar's recent historical accounts are clearly meant as attacks on the Hindu revivalist movement in India, which the communists have always regarded as their main enemy. As Hindu revivalists are emphasizing the continuity of the religion and the ongoing relevance of its traditions, Thapar and her associates are looking for ways to deny it.

Marxists like Thapar like to appear as social liberals and objective academicians and some intellectuals trained in the Western tradition may look at them in this light. Thapar does not parade her Marxism, particularly in recent years, and her criticism of Hinduism, though harsh, is presented in an indirect scholarly style, which makes it less obvious. But we should understand the background of such thinkers, which is hardly objective or free of political motives.

I am conscious of the fact that the subject is big and my treatment of it is sketchy. I am, for example, not discussing at all the tie-up of Marxists in Indian universities with Marxists in European and American universities, how the two stand together and by each other, how the Indian Marxists have found hospitality in Western universities, and so on. What I am pointing out is that simply because a don comes from India does not mean that he or she is providing an accurate or sensitive account of Hinduism or the history of India. In fact, Indian scholarship often tends to be very second-hand, and Indian scholars, in the absence of a perspective of their own, tend to be imitative. I must say that the most Westernized, anti-religious, materialistic intellectuals I have ever met were in India, not in the West, and they were often teachers in universities. The same inability to understand or even appreciate religion can be said of many professors in America, who as products of materialistic Western academia are similarly likely to analyze religion not as a spiritual phenomenon but as a purely social-political institution. Leftist scholars in India look to such Western thinkers for their inspiration and have little regard for the Hindu spiritual and philosophical tradition which they neither understand nor feel any kinship with. If they have any God or guru, it is Marx, and Hindu systems like Vedanta are as foreign to them as they are to any non-Hindu.

Hindus who are religious—and the great majority are strongly religious—should not mistake such Marxist views for an objective pursuit of truth, whether they come from India or elsewhere. Fortunately with the downfall of communism in the world, the influence of communism in India is on the wane, but just as the old communists are holding on to their declining power in the political institutions of China (and Bengal), they are holding on in the educational institutions of India. It is unlikely that they will let go of their power but fortunately they are dying off and few new students are taking up their line of thought.

As a Westerner writing on Hinduism in a positive light it is strange that the main opponents I have run into are Hindus themselves, that is the Marxist Hindus, who like many rebels are the most negative about their own cultural traditions which they have but recently abandoned. The views of these leftists are often on par with the anti-Hindu views of Christian fundamentalists. While the latter see Hinduism as a religion of the devil, the former see it as a personification of social evil, the manifestation of caste division which is their devil (though curiously Marxism works to encourage class hatred, not to promote social harmony and peace between the classes).

Hindus today, like followers of other religions, should no longer accept the Marxist view of their religion and their history, but to do so they must first unmask it. This does not mean that Hindus have done no wrong or that they should not reform their social system or become more compassionate. The proper social changes that need to be done in India or anywhere else in the world do not require rejecting religion in the true sense, or adapting communist-socialist policies which are failing everywhere. On the contrary, the appropriate changes follow from a better understanding of the spirit of universality in Hinduism, which is the essence of its religious view, its recognition of God as the Self of all beings.

Observing such Marxist thinkers one is reminded of the Katha Upanishad: "Living in the midst of ignorance, considering themselves to be wise, the deluded wander confused, like the blind led by the blind. The way to truth does not appear to a confused immature mind, deluded by the illusion of wealth (materialism). Thinking that this world alone exists and there is nothing beyond, they ever return again and again to the net of Death." The Upanishads saw long ago that materialistic thinkers who regard that this world is the only reality only lead us to ignorance and sorrow. It is about time that people in India started to heed the words of their ancient sages, even if it means questioning modern professors.

1.6
India and the Concept of Nation-State

India has been criticized for not succeeding in becoming a unified and disciplined modern nation-state like Japan and Germany. The ongoing disunity and separatist movements within the country appear to attest to this fact. However the problem is not as simple as this comparison might suggest. India is a subcontinent like Europe, not a small country like Germany. If India has had difficulty in maintaining its unity, it has done better than Europe, which even today is divided into various small states, much as if as the states of India were independent countries.

The European concept of nation-state originally reflected small countries that were homogenous in terms of culture and population, like Germany, France, and England. It was a narrow idea of nationhood with a short history, creating nations out of countries whose existence could only be traced back for a few centuries, and which encompassed small land masses and a limited group of people, generally those belonging to the same ethnic group and speaking the same language. Such narrow nation-states fragmented the subcontinent of Europe and caused two world wars. This nation-state idea could never work for a larger region like India, China or the United States and has long become regressive in the European context. Europe has had to work hard to counter the divisions and prejudices this idea of nationhood has created. Europe is only now uniting gradually and tentatively on economic grounds.

Besides such small nation-states Europe did have empires but these were basically an imperialistic rule of one nation-state over others, not an integrated culture encompassing the subcontinent. The great intellectuals of Europe like Voltaire and Goethe looked to a greater European identity, but their ideas could not win in the political arena because of the ascendancy of the nation-state idea. Europe failed through history in uniting as a subcontinent, though some attempts in this direction were made (for example, Napoleon).

The only country of comparable size that has better succeeded than India through history in maintaining its unity as a country is China. Yet China has a lesser diversity of peoples than India, with the Han Chinese making up 95% of the population, and China has often resorted to violence and even genocide to maintain its central rule. For example in recent times, China has strictly controlled its Islamic population and repopulated much of its Western Islamic area with Han Chinese people, so that the Muslims are becoming a minority in their own region. It is doing the same repopulation with Tibet. While China may have succeeded better than India in maintaining the unity of a larger nation-state, it has succeeded only through the power of brute force, which most Indians are not likely to emulate or want to see happen in their country.

Islamic countries have also failed in producing any large nation-state like India, China or the United States. The Islamic world consists of various small states like Iraq, Iran or Saudi Arabia, which are generally military dictatorships or medieval-style monarchies, often at war with one another. The only type of larger state the Islamic world produced were religious empires, not states defined by a geographical region or common culture. Islam has failed in producing any real secular state or uniting any subcontinent into a country.

The United States has succeeded in maintaining unity over a

wide region mainly because it was populated by immigrants from distant lands and did not have to deal with any long established identities of peoples in its own country. It also massacred or relocated the indigenous people, the native Americans. Japan, like Germany, is a small country with a single ethnic group, which makes unification much easier. We see therefore that developing a unified but diverse culture throughout a subcontinent, such as India is attempting, has not really been accomplished anywhere in the world today.

The main problem India has had in recent times is with its Islamic minority, which brought about the partition of the country in the first place. However there has not been another country which has a significant Islamic minority that has not had trouble with it either (for example Israel, Yugoslavia, the Soviet Union, or China). The problem appears to be more an Islamic problem than an Indian one. It goes back to the Islamic rejection of the division of religion and state and the Islamic division of humanity into the rule of Islam (which is thought to be the will of God) and the rule of non-Islam (which is regarded as unholy and to be replaced by the rule of Islam).

India has not yet gone through a nationalistic phase like modern Europe. It has not had a period like modern Europe wherein the different states within India functioned as different countries or regarded themselves as different nations. Foreign rulership helped prevent this from occurring, but a tendency toward it still remains. Part of the fragmentation in modern India has occurred because parts of the country, like Tamil Nadu for example, are trying to undergo a nationalistic phase. It is easy to observe from Europe that such small nation-states wreak havoc upon a subcontinent and if India were to divide into them it would have similar wars, genocides, and relocations of populations followed by a longer term seeking for reunification along economic lines as has been the case with Europe. Hopefully India will not have to go through the European style nationalistic phase, and the results if it did would be disastrous.

Therefore the concept of nationhood needs to be revised today, not only in the case of India but owing to the problems nationalism has caused all over the world. The great countries of the future will not be narrow nation-states in the nineteenth century European style model. They will be unified subcontinents or large geographical regions that have an organic unity in their common land and culture. Only those parts of the world which succeed in creating such greater nations will prosper in the twenty-first century. India, China, the United States, Brazil, Australia are regions of such size which have the capacity to prosper in this way. Europe is realizing this and moving in a similar direction. Smaller nations will end up dependent upon the larger ones as they cannot possibly be self-sufficient economically or technologically.

That India has failed to become a nation like Germany or Great Britain is only to be expected. What India needs is to create a broader model of a country than such narrow nationalism allows. This requires recognizing the need of maintaining unity through the diverse cultural and economic basis of the Indian subcontinent, but a unity which integrates the diversity rather than suppressing it. This agrees more with the nature of Indian civilization which, based upon the Hindu religion and all of its diversity, has always been synthetic in nature.

Such a redefinition of nationalism is not only what India needs but also the rest of the world. This broader concept of nationalism leads to internationalism, to a global approach in which the various geographical regions of the world can be brought together into the larger organic unity that includes the entire planet. To create this is the challenge of all present governments but it requires a spiritual view to really develop. Perhaps India can pioneer this if it can awaken to its inner potential.

1.7
Religious Persecution in Pakistan

Reuters news agency reported that "Local authorities in Rawalpindi on Thursday, 15 September 1994, razed the structures of a place of worship of the banned Ahmadiya sect of Islam." Local authorities means the Pakistani government. Rawalpindi is located next to Islamabad, the national capital, meaning that the national government must have been aware of the event and allowed it.

The Ahmadiya mosque had been functioning for over fifty years. There was no dispute that the place belonged to the Ahmadiyas. It was not an issue of property. The issue was that orthodox mullahs are opposed to the existence of any Ahmadiya mosques in Pakistan, not that they were disputing the location of one of them. Nor is this the first Ahmadiya mosque to be destroyed in Pakistan. Ahmadiyas report over a dozen mosques destroyed throughout Pakistan since the Ahmadiyas were declared illegal by the Pakistani government of General Zia in 1984. The destructions have generally been carried out by the Pakistani police, incited by orthodox mullahs. In addition, Ahmadiya leaders have fled the country, as under current Pakistani law they can be imprisoned for three years, merely for performing Islamic practices or claiming to be Muslims. Some Ahmadiya leaders who have stayed in Pakistan have been murdered for their beliefs.

The Ahmadiya sect dates back to the nineteenth century and numbers four million in Pakistan and up to ten million throughout the world. Ahmadiyas are accused by orthodox Muslims as being unorthodox for regarding their founder as a prophet on par with Mohammed, which is considered heresy for orthodox Muslims who, though they recognize a variety of prophets to have existed before Mohammed, regard Mohammed as the last prophet and do not accept that any more prophets can come after him. Ahmadiyas deny this attribution, also honor Mohammed and the Koran, and follow the Sharia or traditional Islamic law. But Ahmadiyas do recognize their founder, Mirza Ghulam Ahmed (1835-1908), as the Messiah whom all Muslims are looking for (who therefore cannot be regarded as a prophet to compete with Mohammed).

The destruction of the Ahmadiya mosque reveals the fact of religious oppression in Pakistan. While the oppression of non-Muslims, particularly Hindus and Christians, is a normal principle in Islam—especially the destruction of Hindu temples in Pakistan—this event shows that even unorthodox Muslims are not tolerated. The goal of Pakistan appears to be to gradually eliminate all religious groups but orthodox Sunni Muslims. Dissent is not allowed within Islam, much less outside of it.

This event has several important ramifications. First of all it shows that there is no real religious freedom even for its own kind in Pakistan, which now resembles a fundamentalist state wherein only one form of Islam is accepted. The mullahs appear on the verge of taking power as in Iran. Pakistan's appearance as being a democratic state is shown to have no real validity. Second it shows that the international community is not very concerned about religious oppression in Pakistan or other Islamic countries. We are reminded of Saudi Arabia in which no religions are allowed except the Saudi version of Islam and yet no Western country complains or threatens sanctions against Saudi Arabia to improve its dismal human rights record. In fact the

Saudis have sided with Pakistan against the Ahmadiyas and will not allow them into their country either.

With all the talk of human rights in the world, particularly by the United States, it is strange that such events occur without the slightest response by those who claim to be concerned about the welfare of all people. Human rights policies are shaped by political and economic interests, including the power of petro-dollars and global arms sales. The United States, the self-proclaimed great champion of human rights, is also the greatest seller of arms in the world and its best buyers are Islamic countries.

In addition the demolition draws comparison with the destruction of Babri Masjid or Babar's mosque by Hindu groups in India during December 1992. For demolishing a disputed site that the Hindus looked to as the birth place of the avatar or Divine incarnation, Lord Rama—which had not been used as a mosque for over fifty years but which has been used for regular Hindu worship—four of the state governments in India were dismissed and the largest Hindu organizations in the country were banned. Protests over the event were directed at India from most Islamic countries.

However should Muslims destroy the mosque of another Islamic sect in a far more dramatic way, nothing happens and no one notices the event, much less protests. Muslims, it appears, can destroy mosques and it is alright, but no non-Muslim group can touch a mosque or the Islamic world will rise in protest against them.

Had it been Hindus who destroyed such a mosque as that in Rawalpindi, the response would be similar to that of Babri Masjid. Yet even the Hindu groups who demolished Babri Masjid were not expressing a desire to eliminate all mosques from the country but only to reclaim one of their holy sites. Hindus were not opposed to mosques as such, but with a mosque—placed they claim by force on a Hindu temple destroyed by Islamic armies—on what Hindus regard as one of their most holy sites in one of their sacred cities. The Pakistani move was not to reclaim any particular place but simply to eliminate the places of worship of a non-orthodox sect.

The destruction of this Ahmadiya mosque reveals the pattern of destruction of non-orthodox Islamic and non-Islamic holy sites in Pakistan. Hindu temples in Pakistan have been routinely taken over or destroyed since the partition of the country. In fact some sixty places of Hindu worship were destroyed or damaged in the days that followed the demolition of Babri Masjid and with no evident remorse by the Pakistani news media or government. Even in Kashmir it is the Sunni Muslims who are leading the terrorist action against India, and it is not only Hindus but Buddhists, Sikhs, Ahmadiyas and Shia Muslims who are among those whom they attack and want to eliminate. Should the Sunnis take over Kashmir, these other religious groups are bound to disappear ignominiously.

Strangely today India has become home for the largest number of Islamic sects in the world, more than any Islamic country. The reason is that most Islamic countries are enforcing a Sunni type orthodoxy upon the population, with the exception of Iran, which is imposing a Shia orthodoxy on its population, and trying to eliminate all other Islamic groups. Hence Islamic groups like the Ahmadiyas have taken refuge in India where there is greater religious freedom. The same is true of the Bahais, a Shia sect, who originated in Iran, an Islamic country. If India did not exist as a place of refuge, these Islamic sects might be in danger of extermination.

It has to be found out if the fact of their being persecuted in Islamic countries and finding safety in a Hindu majority country has made any difference to their view of Hindus and Hinduism. The Ahmadiyas for instance are known to have been zealous missionaries of Islam for converting Hindus, and in the forefront of the demand for Pakistan. One wonders if their present situation in Pakistan on the one hand and India on the other has occasioned some rethinking on their part. For all we know, these persecuted sects may repeat the story of Syrian Christians who had found refuge in India from persecution at the hands of their co-religionists but who rallied round the Portuguese persecutors of Hindus after having enjoyed Hindu hospitality for several centuries. Hindus have to address themselves to this curious phenomenon of the persecuted sects retaining the persecution mentality inculcated by a parental closed creed.

Hindus meanwhile should recognize by such events the dangers that exist to members of their religion in Islamic countries, which have no qualms about suppressing religious minorities. If Hindus don't learn to speak out against such oppression, it is going to continue without question and, therefore, without change, because clearly the global media does not care very much either.

1.8 Taking Offense At One's Religion Being Criticized

Many Muslims are offended should anyone criticize their religion, particularly if this criticism comes from those who were born Muslims, as the case of Taslima Nasreen in Bangladesh once more brings to light. Nasreen has said that the Koran needs to be thoroughly revised. Later she added that the Koran should be regarded as an historical document only and is now out of date. Nasreen, if convicted for the crime she has been accused of by the state, will get two years in prison merely for criticizing Islam. A price has also been put on her head by Islamic fundamentalist groups in the country, who are demanding that she be hanged. Not surprisingly she has fled the country, which obviously does not appear to be a safe place for her, or anyone who might question the majority religion of the land.

Muslims throughout the world have asked for the ban of a number of books, written by both Muslims and non-Muslims, and have even demanded the execution of authors like Salman Rushdie who have criticized Islam, with only a small number of Muslims appearing to take a stand to the contrary. Laws against criticizing Islam (anti-blasphemy laws) are found not only in Bangladesh but in Pakistan, Saudi Arabia and the Gulf Countries, in fact in most Islamic countries, as such laws are part of traditional Islamic legal codes which these countries subscribe to by declaring themselves to be Islamic republics. Anti-apostasy laws are also found in most of these countries, which forbid Muslims from becoming non-Muslims, sometimes at the cost of their lives.

Yet it is interesting to note that non-Islamic countries have also taken to banning books against Islam, particularly if these countries contain a significant Islamic minority, even if such bans go against the secular nature of their constitutions and their laws of free speech. India, a country that has historically suffered from numerous invasions and destruction by Islamic armies, was the first country in the world to ban Salman Rushdie's *Satanic Verses* for its criticism of Islam, and Salman Rushdie was a citizen of India! Nor has India done anything to help Taslima. Such countries do not take a similar action against those who criticize religions other than Islam, including the majority religions of their lands. They are placating Islamic fundamentalism either for votes, for economic or diplomatic reasons, or out of fear of reprisals or Islamic terrorism.

Many Muslims appear to believe that in seeking such bans they are only asking what Christians or those of other religious backgrounds would require in their countries, should their holy books be criticized. However if we look into the matter we see that there are many books which criticize Christianity, Judaism, Hinduism and in fact all the religions of the world at least as vehemently as the books that Muslims feel so offended about for criticizing Islam.

Many of the most famous intellectuals of Europe have written scathing remarks on the church, the Bible or Christ himself. Such figures include great writers and philosophers of various countries over several centuries including Voltaire, Goethe, Nietzsche, Bertrand Russell, Sigmund Freud and J. Paul Sartre, to mention but a very view. They include communist philosophers and politicians like Marx, Engels, Lenin, and Mao-tse Tung (though curiously the communists of Bengal have refused to support Nasreen in her cause) and many of the founding fathers of the United States, like Thomas Jefferson and Thomas Paine, who did not consider themselves to be Christians. Thomas Jefferson writes that "the Bible God is a being of terrific character, cruel, vindictive, capricious and unjust." Thomas Paine writes of the Bible that "it would be more consistent that we call it the work of a demon than the word of God."

If Christians insisted that books which criticized their faith or holy book had to be banned, such as Muslims are doing today, thousands of books would have to be banned, including many of the most famous literary and philosophical works in the West. If any one who says such remarks about Christianity as Rushdie or Nasreen has said about Islam should be executed, thousands if not millions of people would have to die. If anyone who said that the Bible should be thoroughly revised had to be sent to prison, there would not be enough prisons in the world to hold those making such remarks in one Western country.

The situation is yet more complex. It is not merely non-religious people who have criticized religions, different religions have also criticized each other. Should the Bible be banned, for example, because it offends the sentiments of Pagans, of whom there are still existing groups in Europe and America, by branding them as instruments of the Devil and thereby promoting social discrimination against them? You may laugh at this, but are Pagans not also people and don't they have their human rights? Hindus are often lumped together with these so-called Pagans as ungodly people, and have been historically subject to the same oppression. In fact during the last thousand years of Islamic and Christian attacks against them Hindus have endured, generally passively, more aggression, intolerance, and genocide than any other religion in the world. Are members of these other religions, particularly Islam, willing to hear the complaints of Hindus against them?

In this regard we should note that the Koran itself contains many statements that are offensive to the sentiments of non-Muslims. The main daily prayer of Islam—which is broadcast by loud speakers at mosques in Islamic and non-Islamic countries—that there is no God but Allah and Mohammed is his final Prophet, is offensive to non-Muslims. It implies that those who worship God or Truth other than under the name Allah, or those who follow another religious leader than Mohammed are wrong and evil. It invalidates all religions founded after the time of Mohammed, like the Sikh or Bahai. Moreover, like the Bible, the Koran proclaims that those who use idols in their religious worships are unholy and implies in many places that they should be converted by force if necessary. This offends all those who use images and idols in their religious worship, like the Hindus, Buddhists, and Taoists as well as Native American, African, and Pagan European religious groups, who have often through history been the target of Islamic and Christian aggression, for which the justification often given has been such remarks in these scriptures.

Moreover religions have criticized non-religious people, and often unfairly. Should religious books criticizing atheists be banned, because atheists are offended by them. This should be the case if the criticism of religion by atheists should be banned. Don't atheists have equal human rights in a secular government?

We live in a pluralistic world that contains many different religions and many people who do not follow any religion at all. Unless we want to give up social freedom and humaneness, we have to let people of different religious views coexist, which means also to allow them to criticize each other, as long as they don't try to physically harm others or force their views upon them. There are secular law codes about slander and libel that can be resorted to if criticism is unwarranted or untruthful, which is the proper channel to deal with such problems.

If Muslims are going to proclaim it an injustice to the world when anyone offends them, they must be willing to respect that other groups may also be offended, including by what Islam teaches and by what Muslims say or do. It is not the case that Islam has had a history of not criticizing or offending those of other beliefs, and that Islam therefore should expect no criticism in return. As a conversion oriented religion Islam is highly critical of all other beliefs, and trying to supplant them, sometimes by force. Nor is Islam the only religion in the world, and there are no other religious points of view to consider. Islam is only one religion among many, and it is neither the oldest nor the newest. If Muslims are going to expect books which offend Islam to be banned, they should allow books that offend other religious or even non-religious groups also to be banned, even if they are written by Muslims or by Mohammed himself. Such a process however would be unending and only promote illiteracy.

We all have our sentiments, not just those of us who are Muslims. We all think that our religion or philosophy is the best or we wouldn't be following it. No one likes his or her chosen religion, philosophy or political ideology to be criticized and yet all have been criticized by somebody and sometimes unfairly or inaccurately. Some of us are trained not to be self-sensitive and to recognize that other people see the world differently than we do and that we need not try to impose our views upon them in order for us to feel secure. We choose to challenge criticism by giving our own point of view, not by trying to silence it by the use of force. Religion should encourage broad-mindedness and open-heartedness that can accommodate any number of points of view and remain unshaken before any amount of criticism, however unfair. If we all learn to do this, including in the Islamic world, there will certainly be more peace and understanding between all people.

Banning of books and persecution of authors is a hold over from the dark Middle Ages that is out of place in the modern world or in any humane society. It is not part of any truly religious view which requires not only devotion to God but love of one's fellow human beings. That an author has to live in fear for his or her life for criticizing religion—which after all is supposed to bring us peace and show us a higher way of living than anger, revenge and violence—is a sad thing for everybody, particularly for truly religious people regardless of their belief.

Section II

Religious Issues

2.1
Vedanta, Unity and Universality

The Unity of Truth

"Truth is only One:" thus have the sages declared since the time of the most ancient Rig Veda. If we did not have any sense of this One Truth why would we seek to know anything at all? The sense of an underlying order, harmony or law behind existence is the basis of all systems of knowledge. Even to speak of falsehood or unreality is only possible if one recognizes a lasting truth relative to which it can be compared.

If such a truth or rationale for existence can be found it cannot be a mere material or unconscious force. The very fact that the world is intelligible indicates that its basis is intelligence. An insentient force cannot produce order, nor can it organize itself, much less perceive itself. There must be a universal power of consciousness for there to be any order to the world and to the movement of the forces which constitutes it.

And if this One Truth is a power of consciousness, how can it be apart from our own awareness? How can any cosmic consciousness be separate from the consciousness of the individual? How could any form of life or mind be excluded from it? Therefore the One Truth must reside within us and within all beings. It cannot be something peripheral or extraneous to who we are, but must dwell at the core of our being as the underlying power of consciousness itself. Truth cannot be other than our true nature. We can only find peace of mind when we have discovered that Truth and come to live according to it, which is to live in it as our real Self.

The unity of Truth is the fundamental principle of the Vedantic system of philosophy which has dominated India since ancient times. A similar intuition of unity occurs to some degree in the nobler aspirations of all human beings regardless of time and culture, though it has not always been proclaimed as clearly and logically as in Vedanta. Yet the unity of Truth is not merely a philosophical theory or a religious belief. It reflects the highest and most direct experience—that of our own consciousness itself divested of all limiting preconceptions in which we discover all the universe, all beings to exist within ourselves. If there is only One Reality can we be other than it?

If we affirm that God or Truth is One and then proclaim that we or others are apart from it, have we not contradicted ourselves? To affirm that Truth exists is to acknowledge that it is part of our own being. Once the mind is cleared of its conditioning this unity of Reality shines forth like the sun divested of the clouds. All those who have purified their minds through the practice of deep meditation realize this Oneness of the universe. To discover it we must value the life and teachings of those who have realized it, and shape our action and behavior accordingly. It cannot be arrived at through the mind alone but only through the totality of our life and our every action.

The Nature of Truth

What is the ultimate Truth that all human beings seek? The mind is only satisfied with a Truth that never fluctuates or ceases to be valid. Truth is that which is eternal, consistent, self-evident and absolute. It cannot change its nature or it would not be Truth. For example, the true quality or property of fire is that it burns. Fire cannot cease to burn without ceasing to be fire.

What then is the true quality or property of the human being?

It is not our possessions which are transient. It is not our titles, which similarly pass away through time, nor our bodies which are born and die, or our minds that are constantly changing. Nor is it our various national, racial, sexual or religious identities, which are similarly limited within the field of time and shift according to circumstances. Our true nature resides in our awareness of Truth, our consciousness of the Eternal and the Infinite as the fact of existence. That alone in us has the power to go beyond death and the power to overcome the forces of division and destruction that abound in this transient world. Only what has no form, what transcends materiality and circumstances, can be ultimately real or true. Yet what has no form is not any mere emptiness or vacuum but the immaterial nature of consciousness itself.

Unity and Universality

The statement that Truth is only One does not mean that Truth has only one name or can be expressed in a single formulation. It is not a statement of limitation or qualification on Truth. That Truth is One also means that it is universal, innate in all beings and inherent in all existence. Truth is both one and infinite, which means beyond all boundaries and definitions. It cannot be circumscribed by any belief, idea or personality, however great these may be.

That Truth is only One also means Truth has any number of formulations or expressions and cannot be reduced to any single one of them. The unity of Truth is an inclusive unity, not an exclusive singularity which cannot accept anything but itself. Truth is not one thing opposed to another but that which transcends and includes within itself all things. Truth is like the ocean which can accept all streams without being increased or decreased. To uphold the unity of Truth correctly we must affirm its infinity and universality and not limit it to any human formulation. Truth is not a thing of the marketplace, nor some form of information, someone's opinion, or any form of dogma or propaganda. It is found in the nature of existence, and cannot be reduced to any external form or expression. It transcends all organizations and classifications.

Truth is not a mere material thing that can be possessed by anyone. It cannot be owned by any particular group, institution, or culture. No one can control, dispense, or rule over it. It is beyond all saviors, prophets, holy books, churches, and temples. Truth is an internal perception, not an external structure. It is an individual realization not a collective phenomenon.

Truth therefore resides in our own direct experience of Reality and not in any external place or person. It cannot be given to us by another, nor can any other person, whatever they may do, substitute for our own contact with the Truth. Though others may guide us to Truth, and such guidance is usually essential, the ultimate goal is the freedom of our own Self-awareness, not subjugation to a particular belief or group. The ultimate Truth belongs to the individual in his or her communion with the reality of being both within and without.

Today people, particularly in the Western world, are worried about the influence of cults, especially on their children. Actually whatever teaches us that truth lies outside ourselves—that truth is not inherent within us but rests upon some external savior, church or holy book—is a cult or a mystification. Truth transcends all externalities and should never be made hostage to any of them or it is not truth but illusion.

Toward a Spiritual Science

From the scientific point of view, we all live under the same universal laws. Gravity functions the same for all people regardless of age, sex, race, religion or culture. The rains do not fall according to political or religious boundaries, nor does the wind stop at the border. The great forces of Mother Nature do not function according to human opinions and their various prejudices of caste and creed. There is only one Truth governing the entire universe of mind and matter. Yet most of the time we miss this one Truth, simple though it may be, and become caught in the various glittering phenomenon of the external diversity that arise from it.

Just as there is only one science based upon the unity of physical laws for all human beings, so there must be only one religion based upon the unity of spiritual laws for all creatures. There are not different sciences for different peoples, races, cultures, or religions. There is not a Russian science as opposed to an American science, or a Christian science as opposed to a Buddhist science. There is not one set of physical laws for people of one religious belief or identity and another set for those who think differently. Fire is not wet and water dry for some people, while fire is hot and water wet for others. The elements do not change their nature according to our opinions or speculations. So too real religion cannot be different, though like science, religion should remain a diverse phenomenon and an inquiry into Truth rather than the imposition of a particular dogma.

Based on recognizing the unity of physical laws governing the universe all scientists share the same knowledge and look for a truth that stands on reason and experiment and does not cater to personal, social, or cultural biases. In the same way, people of all religions must examine their beliefs and ideals and find out what is really valid within them. We must learn to treat the different religions of the world, whether they have many adherents or only a few, from the standpoint of the one religion of Truth. The different religions of the world are no different than various scientific laws and theories. They must be subject to the same scrutiny to see how and if they work. We must examine them objectively, though with care as in examining a subtle object under a microscope, and find out to what extent or in what manner they may be true, not merely in theory but in practice.

In this way we will discover that some religious ideas are

true for all peoples and all times, others are partially true, and yet others are not true at all or, at best, an inferior truth valid only at a certain level. In science, Newtonian physics describes ordinary physical laws well but it breaks down when dealing with elemental forces, in which quantum mechanics becomes more significant. Similarly religious beliefs for ordinary levels of human life break down when we examine the deeper levels of the mind. Outward moralistic or ritualistic religious beliefs, with their rewards and punishments, must be replaced with an inner way of meditation to free the mind from its conditioning and realize our true nature. Otherwise our religions remain on a childish level and we have not yet really addressed the spiritual potential of humanity.

Vedanta and Religion

Vedanta is such a spiritual science of the highest order. It aims at connecting us with the universal Truth, and it does not stop short at limited, partial, or preliminary truths. Vedanta examines all the beliefs and practices of its own Hindu tradition, and finds that only some of them represent the highest truth, whereas others are inferior or partial teachings. Rituals, for example, Vedanta finds to be mainly of value for people at an early stage of spiritual development or as practices for general welfare, while those who can practice meditation are no longer required to perform them.

Vedanta sees the same levels in all the religions of the world, which exist not only to link mankind to the One Truth but also serve various lesser goals of moral upliftment or merely social control. Vedanta takes us to the highest level of religion which is a practical path of Self-realization. This takes us beyond religion, in fact beyond all externalities to our true Self. From the standpoint of Vedanta all forms of knowledge are only aids to Self-knowledge, gaining which we go beyond them, including all religious beliefs. Religion, properly employed, should serve to take us to the point of Self-inquiry, to direct us to the path of Self-knowledge, or such religion is deficient in its usefulness.

The Religion of Truth

Just as there is only One Truth, there is only one true religion, which is the religion of Truth. Everything apart from Truth is not a religion in the real sense of the world—that is, not a means of linking with what is Real—but a form of ignorance or illusion, though it may have some preliminary value or contain useful practices.

Truth is the only true religion. In this regard Truth is even greater than God. If one has to choose between truth and God, one should choose Truth, because even God has to bow down before Truth. God may only be an idea, a concept, or sometimes merely a name or prejudice invented by the human mind, but Truth is the reality that we cannot ignore. The truth of who we are is something that we cannot escape.

The true religion is Truth, but what we call religion is not always truth. In this regard all religious teachings should be put to the test of Truth and only what survives that test should be concentrated on, with the rest discarded as inessential. This will allow us to create a religion for all of humanity that is free from illusion and exploitation. In this regard, we should hold to the Truth, even if it requires letting go of what may commonly be regarded as religion.

Nor is Truth limited to what we call religion or to what exists in the predominant religions in the world today. Truth is found to some degree in all human pursuits of knowledge including science, art and philosophy. Many of the tribal beliefs of so-called primitive people also contain great truths and a living connection with the real universe that is more real than many organized religious activities, which often are not even connected with life, much less with God.

Yet the ultimate Truth is only found when we go beyond all

names and forms, when we remove the veil of appearances and perceive the underlying Existence-Consciousness-Bliss (*Sacchidānanda*) at the heart of all life. This is the message of Vedanta, which is not limited to any religion, philosophy or science but is the ultimate goal of all human striving. Religion is not the end but the means to connecting with our true Reality, which can only be discovered inwardly through profound meditation.

Naturally our interpretations of this One reality vary because each of our minds is different. We each look upon the world from the unique perspective of our mind-body complex and its changing conditions. We see things relative to the limited perspective of our senses. We interpret things relative to the limited views of our minds. We function through the limitations of language. We ourselves are limited entities, in separate vestures (body and mind), confined to time and space and hence trapped in a certain limited perspective that causes us to misperceive reality. However, the Reality itself is not tainted.

Yet in spite of this diversity, and our inability to formulate Truth according to the unity of Reality, that Divine unity persists. Without unity there cannot even be multiplicity. Without the One there cannot be the many. And however much we are trapped in outer appearances we can never accept them as truly real, nor find lasting fulfillment within them. Our soul will search yet deeper for the Eternal Truth that dwells within us.

The Challenge of the Present Age

All true spiritual teachings aim at the realization of Truth in our own consciousness, which is the unification of the individual with the universal Reality. This is the ultimate goal of both science and religion. This truth is clearly and directly presented in the teaching of Vedanta.

All of the problems in the world today arise from an inability to grasp the underlying oneness of life. The division of nations, religions, and cultures comes from this fundamental ignorance, as does our exploitation of the Earth and her resources. Only if we perceive another person as fundamentally different from ourselves can we harm or exploit them. Only if we see the natural world as mere raw material for our convenience can we damage it for our own gratification. If we see our Self reflected in all beings, which is the real truth, we cannot wish any harm to anyone and we treat all things with respect, finding all life to be sacred.

Without addressing this core problem of the failure to understand the unity of life, we cannot expect to solve our other problems. Today it is of utmost necessity that all those who are consciousness of this underlying unity act in such a way as to make others aware of it. This does not necessarily require any overt outer actions but it does require that we make a statement by how we live, if not by what we say.

The great Vedantic teachers of the twentieth century—like Swami Vivekananda, Swami Rama Tirtha, Ramana Maharshi, and Sri Aurobindo to name a few - have presented this supreme truth of Oneness not only in lucid teachings but in the example of their own lives. To discover how to live in harmony with this truth and how to realize it in the modern world we can look to them. We don't have to look to figures who lived many centuries ago or who spoke a language that we cannot understand. The example of these great Vedantic teachers can serve as a beacon for the coming millennium. Yet it is not enough merely to adulate such figures, though we must honor them. More importantly we should follow their teachings in our daily lives, which is to live a life of peace, permeated by the practice of meditation. We must similarly give these great teachers a place of honor in our educational systems and revere them as our true leaders. If we fail to give them the recognition they deserve as the voice of Truth, then we cannot get beyond the problems that we have today.

A culture is the outcome of its leaders and the ideals that

they follow in their lives. Let us look to leaders who have embodied the highest ideal, which is Self-realization. A culture which does not recognize the value of Self-realization cannot endure, nor can it create unity. On the other hand, a culture based on Self-realization can never be overcome by the forces of time. To create such a culture one must bring the message of Vedanta into all of life, which is also to introduce related aspects of Vedic knowledge like Yoga, Ayurveda, and the Sanskrit language. This is to revive a culture of the Dharma, a spiritual field of human growth. To create such a Vedanta that again encompasses all life and is relevant to the entire world is the key to the spiritual transformation of humanity that the coming millennium requires.

2.2

Practical Vedanta, the Real Message of Swami Vivekananda

What was the real message that Swami Vivekananda brought when he came to the West from India in 1893? Some groups in the Western world have honored the centenary of Vivekananda's first visit as a hundred years of Yoga. Those in India are inclined to see Vivekananda's centenary as an anniversary of the revival of Hinduism in the modern world. Yet others view Vivekananda as having started a universal religion synthesizing all the main religions of the world, based on the teachings of his guru, Ramakrishna. These groups have some validity to their points of view, but they do not completely represent the Swami's great message. In addition, other groups in India—including Communists and Christians who appear to have little in common with Vivekananda and the real scope of his ideas—have tried to see in him some justification for their points of view, portraying him as a social reformer, helper of the poor and oppressed or even as anti-Hindu. These views are merely an attempt by such groups to use Vivekananda for their own purposes and cannot be taken seriously.

Vivekananda did frequently speak about Yoga but for him the term was not the central focus of his teaching. He talked very little of asana or yogic postures, which is what Yoga means to most Westerners today and what most Western Yoga teachers teach. He was not primarily an exponent of this physical Yoga but of all the different branches of Yoga.

To Vivekananda the most important teaching for humanity was Vedanta, the summit of Vedic philosophy, which teaches the unity of the Self and the Absolute. Vivekananda emphasized the great Vedantic realization of "I am Brahman" or "I am God" as the highest truth for all people. According to Vedanta, the essence of all science and religion is the knowledge of oneself in one's deeper nature as pure consciousness transcending all time, space and material embodiment. Vivekananda emphasized Jnana Yoga or the Yoga of knowledge, which is the same as Vedanta, the meditation path leading to Self-knowledge.

Bhakti Yoga, the Yoga of devotion, was also very important to him and he was proficient in chants to the different deities of Hinduism like Shiva and Devi. Raja Yoga, emphasizing the development of the will, was significant for him as well. He saw that the gaining control of the will and developing the power of self-determination was key to the growth of mind and character. Karma Yoga or service was not neglected by him either. He emphasized the need to work continually, not only for our own inner growth but for the upliftment of all humanity. His whole life is an example of spiritual work and selfless service. Hatha Yoga, which revolves around asana (yogic postures) and pranayama (breath control), was the least mentioned by him, though he did see its usefulness as a support for the deeper yogic disciplines.

Over the last hundred years many Americans have taken up the physical side of Yoga but few have given the same attention to the spiritual side of Yoga, which leads one to Vedanta. Americans frequently talk of Yoga and exercise, Yoga and health, Yoga and psychology, Yoga and various New Age therapies and practices. Yoga as sadhana or spiritual practice is seldom discussed, much less practiced. In this regard it is important to look back to the teachings of Vivekananda to help align the Western Yoga movement with the spiritual impulse at its original root.

For Hindus, Vivekananda was a great patriot and perhaps the central figure in the modern Hindu renaissance. He spoke proudly and eloquently as a Hindu and encouraged Hindus to honor and promote the traditional spiritual culture of their land. He affirmed the unity of the entire tradition through the Vedas, Puranas, Tantras and modern teachers, as one movement of spiritual realization. Unlike many modern Hindus he did not hide his Hinduism, make excuses for it, or apologize for it. He felt the superiority of the spiritual cultures of Asia, particularly India, over the materialistic cultures of the West. While he recognized the problems of modern India he looked up to the West only for practical help, not for spiritual or religious guidance. He traveled all over the world as a kind of missionary for Hinduism, promoting Hindu culture and values, and regarded its spiritual teachings as valid for all humanity. He was the greatest missionary of modern Hinduism and paved the way for Hindu teachers to travel throughout the world and establish various centers, in which footsteps many have followed.

Yet for Vivekananda the essence of Hinduism was Vedanta, the way of Self-realization, not the Hindu social structure dating from medieval times. Vivekananda was a great reformer against the rigidity of caste, the mistreatment of women, and other social ills that have become associated with Hinduism because of antiquated social accretions that do not truly represent its spirit. Vivekananda showed Hindus that what is wrong with India is not owing to its spiritual and religious tradition but because this tradition has been misunderstood and misapplied. However, Vivekananda was not just a philosophical Hindu, rejecting Hindu culture and history. He also was a great lover of Sanskrit, the Vedas, Hindu music and all of Hindu culture. He did not seek to impose this culture on others but he was happy to share it with all.

Vivekananda was a universalist, who taught that there is only One Truth behind all the religions, philosophies and sciences of the world. He accepted what was good or true wherever he saw it, in whatever religion or culture, from whatever person regardless of their background. He spoke of the good in many different religions, including Buddhism, Christianity and Islam. He admired what was valuable in Western science and philosophy, and praised even atheists for their intellectual contributions, humanism and free thinking.

Yet this does not mean that Vivekananda merely approved of all religions or thought that all religious practices are equal or good. He criticized the dogma and church bound authoritarianism of Christianity and, for this reason, a number of Christians sought to discredit him in the West. In India he worked to counter the influence of Christian missionaries who were trying to convert the country and destroy the faith of Hindus in their own greater culture and spiritual heritage. While Vivekananda admired the sense of brotherhood found within the Islamic community, he also questioned the validity of Mohammed's revelation. He spoke out against the violence perpetuated in the name of Islam, particularly the record of Islam in India and its campaigns of cruelty and mass destruction aimed at destroying Hinduism. He also criticized the materialism of modern European thought and its inability to provide answers to the fundamental questions of human life, death and immortality.

The universal religion that Vivekananda taught was a modernized form of Vedanta and Hinduism with its broad approach to Truth. He did not seek to replace Hinduism with another religion, nor did he make all religions the same. He looked beyond the name of religion to the actual practices and sought the highest spiritual practices for all human beings. He saw Hinduism as the great Mother religion in which all the others could be integrated. He did not regard it as another creed like the rest, but an open tradition capable of harmonizing all creeds.

For Vivekananda Vedanta was not a philosophy to be thought about or discussed intellectually. It was not a teaching to be limited to a select group of sadhus who lived apart from the world. He taught "practical Vedanta," a way of Self-knowledge in daily life. Practical Vedanta for him meant bringing the spirit of Self-realization into all ordinary human affairs and into society. It means independence, free thinking, nobility of character, and respect for the Divine in everyone. It means truthfulness, compassion, integrity, and not compromising with the forces of ignorance and injustice.

According to practical Vedanta none of us are limited or weak. None of us are fallen and in need of redemption. We are not sick, or in need of comfort or healing. We are not this little body or limited mind. We are not even souls, or children of God. We are God. No, we are greater than God. We are, each one of us, the Self of all beings. This entire universe of matter and mind is no more than our shadow. It is beneath our dignity as the master of the universe to be dominated by anger, fear or desire, to want anything or to be the slaves of anyone's opinion. Our true place in life is to manifest the glory of this Self, not to indulge in petty entertainment, in the hoarding of possessions, the pursuit of fame and power, or other lesser goals of life that breed corruption.

Swami Vivekananda was called "the lion of Vedanta." This is perhaps the best way to remember him. He took the teachings of Vedanta and Hinduism and made them appealing to the modern world not by compromising them but by boldly and fearlessly declaring the Supreme Truth they are based on. He took the knowledge of the ancient seers and rishis and placed it in a futuristic language, pointing out the way for humanity to follow in ages to come. To honor Vivekananda therefore means also to recognize and honor the great tradition from which he came and to seek to share that with everyone. But above all it means to practice Vedanta, which is to be the Self, and nothing less, to not be dominated by the world but to uplift the world in all that we do.

2.3

The Unity of Religion and Unity of Truth

An attitude of tolerance, a kind of ecumenical spirit has gained favor with a number of groups today, particularly in India. It states that all religions are one and therefore worthy of equal respect. It often adds that a person can find Truth by following with faith the religious tradition in which he or she is born, whatever it may be. By this view the great religions of the world represent various paths founded by God to bring people to the same realization. The differences between religions are only differences of name and form that have arisen to communicate the same Truth to people of different countries or cultures.

Those who espouse such views may have pictures of Christ or the Pope, Mecca or some Sufi saint, some Hindu or Buddhist deities or gurus, or other icons from different religions. They may honor the holy days of different religions, like celebrating Christmas, the birth of Mohammed, or the birth of Krishna. They may build temples or churches that have sections for all the main religions of the world—a Hindu window, Christian window, Islamic, Buddhist sections and so on. They tell Muslims that it is fine to be a Muslim, Christians that it is fine to be a Christian, Hindus that it is fine to be a Hindu and so forth, that all are equally great and valid religions, almost regardless of whatever sect or branch of the religion the person may belong to.

Hindu or Yoga groups having this view may tell people that

by following their teachings a Christian will become a better Christian, a Muslim a better Muslim, and so on. They tell people that one need not change one's religion in order to practice Yoga but that Yoga will make one better at one's own religion, whatever it is. Sometimes if Christians come to a Hindu espousing this ecumenical spirit and ask how to find God or Truth, they will be told to return to their own religion and try to become better Christians. They will be discouraged from becoming Hindu or adapting more specific Hindu practices. Those holding this view try to avoid criticism of other beliefs and give the impression that all religions, however diverse and contrary they appear, are right. They make it seem that whether one visits Kailas, Mecca or Rome, whether one prays, fasts or practices meditation, it is all part of the same great and true human aspiration for the Divine and none of these approaches are necessarily better than the others.

While much has been said to support this view, it remains a generalization that is not as specific as its proponents would like to believe. It reflects a noble sentiment, a powerful intuition, and a seeking for peace, but it is often pushed so far that it inhibits clear thinking. It can end up equating teachings superficially, mixing up doctrines of different sorts, and discouraging discrimination. To generally recognize human religious aspiration in all its forms is not necessarily to equate these forms or to make them the same. While it is crucial that we unify all religions, this cannot be done by pretending that religions are already one. To discover the real unity behind religion and behind all life is a much greater endeavor that requires a tremendous inquiry and deep examination until we arrive at the core of Truth hidden behind the veil of forms and dogmas.

Some may argue that, though there are differences between religions which can be quite major, it is better to emphasize their common factors, however limited they may be, in order to gradually bring them together. This view is more sound but the goal is not merely to bring religions together but to find Truth. We should not sacrifice Truth, glossing over the differences between teachings, in order to make different religions accept one another, or what they are accepting will only be some convenient partition of humanity into religious camps, not the real Truth in which alone is abiding unity.

That all religions as we know them are one is a pleasant thought and can succeed in bringing together the more open or mystical elements in religions to some extent, but it cannot deal with the deep seated differences between religions. To really unify religions requires finding the universal Truth behind religion. This is as much a matter of transcending religion as we know it as of affirming it. To proclaim the unity of religion without establishing the Truth behind religions can give rise to many wrong perceptions. It can confuse tolerance with Truth and thereby prevent any deeper examination. It can prevent any deeper questioning as to what religion is and where religion should take us.

We certainly should tolerate all religions and respect the Truth wherever we find it. However, this does not mean that we have to put all religious teachings on the same level in order to do so, or that we have to bow down before all religious authorities and institutions. The many differences between religions, like those between cultures also have their beauty, importance and uniqueness. Moreover just as all cultures have not developed all fields of human endeavor to the same degree, so too all cultures have not developed spirituality to the same degree.

Different Paths and Truth

What do we really mean when we say that all religions are one? Have we really gone to the core of Truth or are we merely making a statement that can be acceptable to everyone? Is it merely a slogan designed to cover over the differences between religions so that we can all live together in social harmony without having to question our different beliefs? Is it a political strategy designed to create peace between the conflicting religious groups in a country or in the world? Is it the strategy of new spiritual or religious groups to gain converts for themselves from people of all religious backgrounds? If so, it may not come from a place of Truth that can really unite us.

Do we mean by such a statement that we accept all the differing claims of various religions? Obviously those who truly believe in a unity behind religion cannot accept the dogmatic claims of any one particular religion. For example, if religions other than Christianity are true then Jesus cannot be the only son of God, nor can the Christian heaven and hell be ultimate realities. The same case exists with Islam. If other religions are true then Mohammed cannot be the last prophet or the Koran the final revelation for all humanity. The limited dogmas of all religions, whatever they may be, which reduce truth to a particular name, form, person or institution would not be acceptable. If we scrutinize the matter at all, we see that finding validity in many different religions challenges the claims of religions which consider that they have the sole or final truth. Yet this goes against what most people in some religions believe. If we take the exclusive claims out of many religions we find that the religion, as commonly understood by the great majority who believe in it, is not the Truth.

There is a unity to Truth and to what could be called the spiritual or mystical experience, but this Truth is not equally accepted by all religions, particularly in their commonly understood forms, which may be against mysticism. All religions as they represent themselves in the world today do not recognize the same goal of spiritual enlightenment. Otherwise they would not be fighting for converts or trying to maintain their separate identities.

The unity of religions is an ideal, not a fact, and an ideal that requires considerable reshaping of the actual in order to arrive at.

The obvious fact, that the news demonstrates almost daily, is not that all religions are one but that religions are divided against each another, trying to maintain and expand their followings sometimes by whatever means necessary, even if these are inconsiderate or inhumane.

The fact is that the religions of the world today are very different and often hostile, just as different countries are. Like countries they may make alliances with one another, even targeting a religion that is a common enemy. Such alliances cannot be looked upon as unity in the true sense but may be no more than matters of convenience. While there are common principles that can be used to gradually unite religions, just as those to unite countries, or at least promote tolerance between them, these are rather vaguely defined and not widely accepted by most of the followers of different religions. If religions were really one, the missionary religious activity that is central to certain religions, which aims at conversion, would be unnecessary and would be stopped, which is hardly likely to occur.

Truth indeed is One, like the sun that shines equally on all people. There is not a different Truth for people of different religious beliefs any more than there is a different sun or moon. There are also many paths to Truth both known and unknown. Truth is infinite and can be approached through a great diversity of paths and expressed in innumerable names and forms. It has the room to accommodate any number of teachings and embraces all the universe. But because Truth is One and there are many possible approaches to it does not mean that all religions must be true to the same degree.

That there is some aspect of Truth in all religions does not mean that all that is done in the name of religion is worthy of respect, or that Truth abides only in religions. There is much falsehood in what we call religion that it would be a sin against Truth to accommodate. In addition there are aspects of Truth which are outside of religion in domains of art, science, philosophy and so on—and the whole world of Nature reflects the presence of the Divine. What we call religion in this world neither owns, nor dispenses Truth, whether by any one religion or by all of them put together.

We can compare the unity of religion with unity in other aspects of life. Establishing unity in a field of knowledge like science does not mean establishing identity between all scientific theories or removing any questioning. Because justice is one we cannot say that all the governments of the world are equally good.

Moreover, while there are many paths to Truth, all paths do not lead to Truth. There are many paths that lead to falsehood. Nor do all paths that lead to Truth go all the way, some stop short. Of the paths that lead to Truth some are direct, while others are convoluted and take many detours. A path can only take us in the direction that it leads and as far as it goes. This means a religious teaching that does not recognize the higher Truth of religion, which is Self-realization, cannot lead us there but has to be abandoned along the way.

A superficial sense of the unity of religions fails to set up a universal standard of Truth and makes Truth relative to one's religion, even when religious doctrines and practices are different or contrary. It gives the impression that Truth is merely a matter of religious belief and that whatever is done in the name of religion is right, however diverse or apparently contradictory these practices may be.

It also fails to understand the true spirit of Hinduism or Sanatana Dharma (the Eternal Tradition), which is not a religion based on belief and cannot be represented by any one teacher, messiah, deity, book or practice. There is perhaps a greater diversity of religious practices within Hinduism than outside of it. Making Hinduism into one religion among many narrows down the scope of what Hinduism represents, which is not one religion as opposed to others but an attempt to sustain an open tradition of spiritual and religious practice that is not confined to any belief or dogma.

Appearing to go beyond social prejudices a superficial ecumenicalism caters to the existing names, forms and vested interests that use religion for their own ends. It sanctions organized religion as a way to Truth, when in fact organized religion is generally an obstacle to the pursuit of Truth. It fails to recognize that throughout much of the world, spiritual practices have been possible only outside of the official religions of the land, and that those who have attempted such practices have sometimes paid with the price of their lives—and in many regions of the world continue to be oppressed.

We need not give credence to organized religion in order to appear tolerant and as long as we do so, we may not be promoting Truth but oppression. If there is any greatness in Hinduism it is because Hinduism is not an organized religion, nor is it based on belief. It does not have a single authority, church, or one place to bow down to. It does not say that we can be saved by merely believing in some savior or holy book but that we will only come to a good end if we live righteously, which is in harmony with universal Truth, not according to the dictates of a religious organization and its dogma.

There is a karma for our action that we cannot escape merely by performing our actions in the name of religion. If our religious practices are based upon exploitation we will have to experience the negative results of that action, whatever our religious leaders may tell us. Nor should we allow the name of religion to be used to promote oppression. If someone under the name of a religion—whether our own or that of other people—is promoting what is false or causes harm, we need not passively accept it because it is said to be part of their religion, merely to appear tolerant.

One could argue that if one looks deeply one will find the same Truth of Self-realization and God-realization as the inner core of all religions, including those which appear to oppose these ideas. But when one gives credence to such religions it is not these spiritual practices one gives validity to but to the existing practices and hierarchies within the religions as they are found today, to the religions such as the great majority of their believers accept. Hence it is the unity of spiritual practices that should be emphasized not the formal structures of religions which are frequently opposed to them, but even this has its limits.

Spiritual practices, like any other actions must have their specific results. If we are seeking to climb a mountain, several routes are possible, but not all are equally valid. Moreover following a path that leads away from the mountain will never take us to the top, whatever that path may be called. Spiritual practices are like different vehicles. Some are like airplanes, some are like bullock carts. While all may take us somewhere, they are hardly all on the same level or all equally recommended for travel.

For example, while the giving of charity can be good (it can also be evil if it is based upon an attempt to convert others), it cannot take us to the ultimate reality, which requires meditation. Charity and meditation are not equally valid methods of finding Truth. Or, for another example, the eating of meat is tamasic or dulling to the mind. That one's religion may sanction or encourage meat-eating does not stop it from dulling the mind. To promote universality we should not feel impelled to give people the impression that discrimination in their actions is not required. Otherwise we are merely encouraging people to follow the religion that most caters to their prejudices, not the one which encourages real spiritual growth.

Hindu Dialogue with Other Religions

Following such syncretic views Hindus are apt to say that they also accept Christianity, Islam and the other religions of the world. However the acceptance of spiritual knowledge wherever it may come from—and it exists to some degree in all people—should not be confused with accepting the dogmas of all religions. A Hindu, following an open spiritual tradition can honestly say that he or she accepts whatever genuine spiritual knowledge may be found in Christianity, Islam, or elsewhere, but this does not mean that such doctrines in these religions as are contrary to the principles (*dharmas*) of Hinduism, like an eternal heaven and hell, the Bible or the Koran as the only Word of God, Christ as the only son of God or Mohammed as the last prophet are acceptable to Hindus. Otherwise Hindus will give those following these religions the impression that such dogmas are true or that Hinduism sanctions them, when it clearly does not.

For example, when some years ago I as a follower of Hindu based Yoga teachings once told a neighbor, who followed a Christian fundamentalist belief, that I also accepted Christianity, he told me then why don't I accept Jesus as my personal savior and the Bible as the Word of God and stop doing such unchristian practices? When I told him that it was my belief that what Christ originally taught was the same as Hinduism, he said that he didn't believe it and interprets the Bible differently. While I attempted to argue some Biblical verses or statements that suggest mysticism in Christianity, he could easily refute them to his own satisfaction. He ultimately said that if the Christianity I accept is the same as Hinduism then it is not the same Christianity that he or other Christians believe in, so why should I call it Christianity at all? This taught me a lesson and showed me the confusion caused by too simplistically equating different religions.

I have to admit that Christianity as it has developed, and as the great majority of Christians believe, is not something that I, accepting the spiritual teachings of the Hindu tradition, can believe in. I don't think that it is necessary to go to Christian church or to follow common Christian prayers. I can't accept Jesus as my personal savior; in fact I don't see the need of such a savior at all. I certainly don't think that it is necessary to promote conversion of people to Christianity; in fact I think it is usually harmful. I can't look upon Christian leaders like the Pope or Billy Grahman as the ideal religious or spiritual leader or equate them with the great yogis of India. Though I can admire Christ and some of his teachings, I cannot see him as unique, and such spiritual teachings can be found much more clearly and completely explained in the Hindu tradition so that there is no necessity to try to dig them up out of whatever fragments Christianity may have.

So rather than create confusion by saying that I am also a Christian, I merely state what I think is true, even if it goes against what most Christians accept. Let the members of different religions define their religions as they like. It is not my place, who am not formally a member to their religions, to tell them what their religions really mean. However I must tell them what I think is the Truth, even if it is not accepted in their religion as they know it.

Unfortunately Hindus tend to think that people of other religious beliefs honor the mysticism that Hindus see behind all religions, which is rarely the case. Hindus talk to members of other religions as if it were the mystical side of the teaching that these people were following, even though such people may be fundamentalists trying to convert them. This prevents Hindus from understanding other religions or from communicating to them what Hinduism really is. It also makes Hindus vulnerable to be deceived by members of other religions who take a liberal appearance to attract Hindus, not because it represents what they truly believe. We should note that both Christianity and Islam in India have taken on many Hindu elements and that the mysticism Hindus see in these religions generally has its roots in India and is much rarer in the countries wherein these religions predominate.

Hindus don't appear to know how to dialogue with those of other religious beliefs. They think they must either agree with whatever members of other religions propose (interpreted in a Hindu mystical light) or that they must ignore them and go their own way, keeping to themselves, and not expressing any contrary opinions (as if different religions were like sovereign nations). Hindus appear to think that it is a sin to disagree with non-Hindus on religious matters, however much Hindus may disagree among themselves, and however much non-Hindus may criticize Hinduism! This is curious because classical India was the opposite. Spiritual and religious teachings of all types were critically scrutinized, examined in detail, and questioned on all levels, such as we find in the various systems of Indian philosophy Hindu, Buddhist and Jain.

Hindus should be capable of having a dialogue with those of other religious beliefs without either agreeing with them or having to turn away. It is not wrong for Hindus to state what they believe is true, even if other groups may not accept it. Nor is it wrong for Hindus to criticize the practices of other religions, if they don't agree with them. In fact the Hindu point of view with its greater respect for life and Nature is much needed to bring real spirituality into the world. Hindus should be friendly and considerate in their communication with non-Hindus, yet they can do so without having to surrender their opinions or to go along with whatever non-Hindus say. Such debate occurs in all fields of knowledge and was always promoted by the great Hindu sages. Hindus should reinstate it today, not just bringing different groups together to agree with one another, but to openly examine religion and spirituality so that the real Truth behind it can be known for the benefit of all.

Some Hindus think that it is against Hinduism to criticize other religions and that all the great modern teachers of Hinduism taught a complete equality of all religions. Let them read such teachers as Aurobindo and Vivekananda more carefully, who were quite critical of Christianity and Islam. They both tried to resurrect the ancient Truth of Hinduism and to project it in a modern way. They were not content for their Western disciples to merely continue the religious practices they were already following but inspired them to take on practices that their own religions considered heretical.

Let them note the example of such great sages as Ramana Maharshi, who never visited any churches or mosques, though they existed in the very town wherein he lived, though he did live and do his practices in the local temple for some years. Ramana Maharshi stated that religion in the ordinary sense is only necessary to take us to a path of Self-realization, after which it can be set aside. This draws into question religions that do not direct us to Self-realization or recognize it as their goal. These teachers saw a unity of truth in the Self of all, but they did not bow down to all the religious institutions and dogmas in the world. Gandhi also frequently criticized Christian missionary activity in India and the Christian dogmas behind it.

The Religion of Truth

The true spirit of universality is the spirit of Truth and Truth does not bow down to personalities, vested interests or names and forms. The true spirit of tolerance is to promote the Truth, not to compromise with falsehood. According to the Upanishads there are two forces in the universe—the knowledge and the ignorance—and these forces move in opposite directions: to the extent that one is pursued, the other is lost. To sanction religious beliefs based on ignorance as valid ways to Truth is a betrayal of Truth.

This does not mean that we should self-righteously condemn the religious practices of others, or that we should say that Truth is limited to our point of view. We must give ourselves and other people the freedom to discover the Truth. But we must see things as they are, and in our communication tell what we perceive as the Truth. Hence if someone asks us what we consider to be the best way to discover Truth we may be doing them a disservice if we direct them back to the religion they are following, if its practices do not lead to Truth or only do so in a very hesitant manner.

The Truth is that what we call religion, particularly in the Western world, is usually opposed to the real spirit of Truth or Self-realization. In this regard the organized religions of the world may be more mistakes than paths to enlightenment, and at best have preliminary value. Nor should the founding of an organized religion necessarily be looked upon as a sign of greatness in a spiritual personage. Many great saints and sages, including some of the greatest, never founded any religion and many have been entirely forgotten by history. Those whom we regard as the founders of religion, on the other hand, may not have subscribed to the beliefs and practices of their so-called followers.

If Hinduism has any value it is not as a means of giving credence to anything that might call itself religion but to give credence to the individual—the real bearer of the flame of the sacred—to pursue his or her path to enlightenment, without having to bow down to organized religion and its dogma. Hinduism in its true sense is the religion of the individual (Atman or Purusha). It provides tools and practices, like yogic practices and meditation, so that we can come to our own direct experience of Truth or the Divine. Hinduism does not insist upon any particular approach or dogmatic formulation. In this respect Hinduism or Sanatana Dharma regards most of what is called religion on this planet, the setting up of dogma, as fundamentally irreligious. The openness of Hinduism should not be used to sanction the dogmas of other religious groups, though it does not prevent us from respecting the Truth in whatever form we encounter it.

There is no Dharma or religion higher than Truth. The truth is not that all religions are one but that, just as there is only one science, so there is only one religion, the religion of Truth. This religion of Truth is not an organization, nor limited to a particular book, person or name of the Divine. We join it to the extent that we follow the Truth. We fall from it to the extent that we follow the ways of ignorance and division. This religion of Truth transcends all names and numbers and has nothing to do with converts. When we make different religious definitions of Truth equally valid, even if they are contradictory, we are denying the real unity and universality of Truth and making it a slave to human opinion.

In that religion of Truth all the accepted and most prominent religions of today may not be equal or have the same place, nor may they represent the full scope of Truth. Some may have a minor place and other teachings not formally religious may have a more significant value. The temple of Truth cannot be made by making all religions equal but by ending the hold of religious and all other dogma on the human mind.

The book of Truth may not consist of equal selections from the most prominent scriptures of the world today. It may give more weight to teachings not recognized as scriptures or perhaps not even regarded as religious, and regard some of what we consider to be scriptures as not significant. Nor may the vision of Truth interpret the so-called scriptures of the world in the same way as most of those who believe in those scriptures. The book of Truth may in fact have little to do with any set formulation and may be discoverable only to the extent that we are able to go beyond words, names and identities.

It is necessary to revive the religion of Truth, not to sanction religious beliefs of all kinds. This religion of Truth is Sanatana Dharma or the Eternal Religion, which is the real name of Hinduism, and the only foundation upon which any religion possesses validity. To reestablish it we must set up universal truths, like the evolution of the soul through the cycles of rebirth, and a spiritual science, like the practice of Yoga and meditation. This requires that we go beyond religious teachings which do not acknowledge such truths.

Whether fire burns or not, for example, is not a matter of one's belief. If a person believes that fire doesn't burn we don't have to give equal weight to that belief in order to appear socially or intellectually tolerant. Yet that is the kind of practice we may be doing in the religious realm if we accept all religious beliefs as valid or equal. The standard of belief is arbitrary and places things beyond examination. To cater to it, even in the guise of tolerance, prevents the process of examination whereby we are really able to discover what is true.

It is necessary to affirm Truth both in religion and outside of it, not merely to affirm religion as we know it as Truth. Such is the real spirit of tolerance and universality but it may require abandoning rather than upholding the religions that we have in the world today. All that we call religion requires a reformulation in the light of universal Truth. Hinduism, as perhaps the most universal of religions, can provide important keys how to do this.

2.4
The Unity of Religion and Religious Tolerance

Those today who like to proclaim that all religions are one, seldom define what all religions have in common. And when they do define these things they may not really be common to all religions. Generally those who believe in the unity of religions say that all religions recognize God and have as their goal the realization of God. Those who hold this view often regard the idea of the unity of religions as the basis of religious tolerance and look at those who do not accept it as somehow intolerant or narrow-minded. Let us look at the different religions of the world and see what they really have in common, starting with the idea of God itself.

Do all religions recognize God? God is the term of Western monotheistic religions and implies monotheism—that there is only One God who is the creator of the universe—which is not the view of reality that we find in all religions. The Western monotheistic concept of God is not the same as the Brahman or the Impersonal Absolute of Hindu thought or the Atman or Supreme Self. It is akin to the Hindu concept of Ishvara or the Cosmic Lord but not identical to it. While Hindus may accept God as a term for the Supreme Reality (which they may not define in a Western monotheistic sense), it is very rare that followers of Western religions will use such terms as Atman, Brahman or Ishvara as equivalent to God or Allah (which they would regard as heretical).

Moreover, several religions do not recognize God or a cosmic creator at all. This includes Buddhism which has always criticized Hinduism for postulating the existence of such an entity. Buddhism recognizes a Spiritual Reality or One Mind, but this is quite removed from the Biblical or Koranic God who creates the world out of nothing, as in the case of one Buddhist thinker recently who called the Biblical God "a primitive idea." Jainism, Taoism, Shinto and a number of other religions do not have such a Creator God either but see karma or simply Nature as the creative force. Some Hindu groups like Sankhya are not theistic either.

Many religions, including Hinduism, have a multiplicity of deities or names and forms for Spiritual Reality. This is also not accepted by monotheistic religions, which have branded religions that are not strictly monotheistic as polytheism and idolatry, and thereby heretical or sinful.

Rather than saying that all religions are based upon a recognition of God—which is not at all true—it is more accurate to state that all religions recognize a Spiritual Reality, which may be called variously God, Allah, Buddha, Shiva, Vishnu, Tao, or any number of names according to the particular system involved. This Spiritual Reality may be defined according to monism, monotheism, pantheism, polytheism, or any number of ideas or made to transcend all ideas. There is hardly any universality for the term God or the concept of monotheism in all religions. To build the unity of religions around the idea of One God can cater to the prejudices of monotheistic beliefs, which would like to regard themselves as the universal factor in religion, when they are only one religious approach.

All religions stress the need to relate to a Spiritual Reality but, just as their difference in names and concepts, they are hardly unanimous what the correct relationship is. Just as their differences about the nature of Spiritual Reality all religions do not share the same goal of their practice. Most religions do not regard union with God or mergence in Spiritual Reality, which is generally the Hindu view, as their goal. They do not see themselves as paths to God but only as ways of better relating to God, whom they may conceive of as quite different than we mere creatures that He has created. Orthodox Christianity and Islam do not aim at union with God or even consider it to be possible. The Christian goal is to go to heaven, generally with a resurrected physical body, and then dwell in the eternal presence of God and Jesus (who also dwells in a resurrected physical body). The Muslim goal is similar, to go to heaven. God-realization or Self-realization in the Hindu sense is not the goal of these religions and may be regarded as delusions by them. Even a number of mystics, including some Hindu Bhakta traditions, have as their goal not complete union with God but nearness, proximity or being in the same world with Him with some sort of subtle or divine body.

In addition, all religions do not follow the same practices or subscribe to the same ethics, though they all generally stress some idea of the good or holy. For example, the non-violence of Hindu, Buddhist and Jain thought is not accepted by some religions, which regard it as a form of cowardice. Many religions classify the failure to perform particular prayers or rituals, or subscribe to certain religious beliefs as on par with moral depravity—like the Catholic view that it is a mortal sin not to go to church on Sunday, just as theft or murder are mortal sins, or the general Christian view that those who don't believe in Jesus, however otherwise good people they may be, must go to hell. Islamic views are generally of the same order. Nor do all religions have the same view as to what constitutes a religious person or a religious order. For example, several religions, like Judaism, Islam and Protestant Christianity, do not have monastic orders and have been opposed to them or regarded them as unholy. While most religions have some form of prayer or ritual, the yogic and meditational practices of Hinduism are rarely found in predominant Western religions, except among mystics who were generally oppressed or branded as heretics (except in the case of Judaism wherein mysticism was generally part of the religion).

The fact is that a person will not get the same realization through all religions as through Hindu paths that teach Self-realization. Many religions neither recognize Self-realization as their goal nor teach methods to achieve it. How could they possibly lead anyone to it, when they don't even recognize it as valid? This explains why such realization as stressed in Vedanta, that of Brahman (the Absolute) or Atman (the Self), is practically unheard of in a number of religions and why in the last two thousand years there are very few figures like the great yogis of India and Tibet who have lived in the Western world, particularly in Western Europe. Otherwise such Westerners as myself, who was raised a Catholic, would not have had to turn to teachers from the East to find teachings that were never given to them in their own religious training.

The most we can say about the commonality of the goal of religions is that all religions direct us to a relationship with a Spiritual Reality as they have conceived It to be, which can be quite variable. The relationship stressed may not be a realization at all—which implies a radical change of consciousness—but conversion to a belief or to a pattern of behavior wherein we maintain our ordinary human and egoic mentality but oriented in a different direction. If it is a mystical experience of the Divine that they seek, it can occur on many different levels and in many different ways and may not be conceived as Self-realization or realization of the Absolute.

The conflicts between various religions have existed at least partly because such differences are inherent within them. Some religions insist upon a personal Creator God as the Supreme Reality, who may be limited to a particular book, savior or prophet. Others look to an impersonal Reality, to a multiplicity of Gods and to a variety of spiritual books or teachings. Some religions are based upon meditation approaches to realize Truth. Others are against them and consider that belief or prayer are sufficient. Some religions are inclusive and try to draw other religions into them. Others are exclusive and try to stand apart in their beliefs from other religions.

If these differences did not exist it would be difficult to explain why religions have had so much trouble with each other through the course of history and why they still have problems today in spite of all the improvements in communication. All the many religious conflicts must go back to something more fundamental than semantics, or merely failing to see that they are all saying the exact same thing in different words, or they would not be so much of a problem. So too, getting beyond these conflicts requires much more than an equation of terminology. It requires looking for a universal spirituality that takes us beyond the religious dogmas in the world today, which still serve to divide humanity into hostile camps.

According to religious synthesizers all religions are the same thing only in a different garb or according to a different name. But is this really true? One can perhaps designate related religions in this manner. For example, one can call Islam Christianity in another garb, though this is a generalization that is not entirely accurate. One can call Buddhism, particularly the Tibetan form, Hinduism in another garb and not be too far wrong. But can one call Buddhism merely Islam in another garb? Can one call Hinduism merely Christianity in a different form? This hardly seems accurate and in fact appears ridiculous. Similarly one cannot honestly call a Hindu temple merely a mosque in another form, or the Koran the Upanishads or the Buddhist Sutras in a different language? Nor can one honestly say that

Mohammed is merely the Buddha in another garb, or Krishna as he appeared relative to the needs of medieval Arabia. Yet this is what we are telling people when we say that there is no difference between these various religious teachers, books, or places of worship.

One can certainly honor and respect many great human beings but this does not require that we equate them with the highest sages. One can honor Mohammed as a mystic, social reformer and political leader but to thereby put him on the same level with great yogic sages like Buddha or Shankaracharya may not be appropriate. One can also honor Einstein, Mozart or Da Vinci and other human beings who were great in various ways, but this does not require making them into enlightened yogis. One can honor different religions and philosophies without having to make them the same or put them on the same level. Christianity has produced many good people and some genuine saints and mystics but it is hardly equal as a religion to Hinduism or Buddhism, which have much more depth, diversity, and wisdom. One can even honor the true idealism behind communism, but this does not require having to make it equal to the great religions. Being open to what is true and good everywhere does not require making all teachings and practices the same.

This idea that all religions are the same covers over the differences within religions themselves. If one says that Christianity can provide a person with spiritual realization, which Christian group are they referring to? Are such different sects as Jehovah's Witnesses, Southern Baptists, and other evangelical and fundamentalist groups on par with the contemplative orders of Catholicism in this regard? Does this mean that we can place Billy Graham on par with the great sages of Hinduism like Ramana Maharshi or with the great saints of Christianity like Saint Francis? To some degree one can equate a number of Sufi doctrines with Vedanta, but does this mean that we should honor the Ayatollah Khomeni equally with Vedantic teachers?

Unfortunately Hindus with a synthetic vision are inclined to attribute similar teachings to other religions —not because followers of other religions accept such teachings—but because Hindus, viewing these religions through the inner vision of Hinduism, read Hinduism into them, seeing it where it may only be vaguely intimated. Those of a mystical bent of mind can read a yogic spirituality into the Bible or the Koran, claiming these books reflect an understanding of karma, reincarnation or even subtle yogic practices. Even if they are right in some instances, this does not change the fact that the great majority of people in these religions do not see such teachings there.

A facile synthetic vision can read a deeper spirituality into the symbols of the Book of Mormon, the preaching of fundamentalist Christians, or various recent New Age channeled books, or even works of science fiction. Those inclined to read spirituality into religious symbols and doctrines can do so everywhere. Does this mean that such inner meanings were always intended, that all these teachings must be equal or that all these teachers were enlightened? If so why should we stop merely with the predominant religions of the world? We can read enlightenment into any of the aspirations of humanity. Some synthesizers have gone so far as to read mysticism into Karl Marx, in which case spirituality loses its meaning altogether and becomes equatable with any sort of idealism or noble sentiment. Such synthesis unites everything by blurring any distinction of higher and lower teachings, which may end up denying the value of the spiritual path altogether.

Religious Tolerance and Freedom

However, that we cannot simply equate all religions does not mean we should not tolerate different religions. Intolerance of other human beings and acts of inhumanity towards our fellow men and women are unacceptable regardless of our religious belief and are contrary to the real spirit of religion or even common courtesy. We should and must tolerate all religions—and also atheism and agnosticism—as different approaches to life that people should be free to follow as long as they don't try to impose their views upon others. Otherwise there can be no peace in the world and we will live not in a free society but in a theocratic police state.

We should be open-minded and large-hearted and allow people the freedom to find Truth. We should be friendly and just with those who have different religious or political views than ourselves, or we are not even kind people, much less spiritual. We should recognize the different levels and temperaments of people and their different views of reality, and that there will always be a number of different types of religions among human beings.

Proclaiming that all religions are one, however, fails to deal with the reality of the differences between them. It tries to whitewash them, when a number of them cannot be reconciled. For example, the law of karma and the cycle of rebirth is either a fact for all people and the idea of sin or salvation leading to an eternal heaven or hell is wrong, or vice versa. Both are not merely different words for the same truth. Pretending that all religions are the same does not really eliminate these differences. It tries to ignore the differences in order to create tolerance. *Such a tolerance will eventually break down when the reality of the differences is discovered.*

On the other hand, if we recognize that there are major differences between religions and allow for freedom in human religious inquiry, then such differences need not become a problem. The clash of ideas in the pursuit of Spiritual Truth, like the clash of ideas in science or philosophy, does not have to become a factor of social conflict, nor do we have to try to stifle it in order to maintain social harmony, which is only to suppress our own intelligence.

What brings about real tolerance is allowing different views to exist, not pretending that such differences do not exist. The point is that *society should tolerate all religions even if all religions are not one and even if some religions are wrong*, and that in society we ourselves should tolerate all religions even if we individually may not agree with them and may oppose them intellectually. What cannot be tolerated is violence used to promote a particular belief, which destroys all tolerance.

True tolerance is based upon respect for freedom, not the assumption that everything tolerated must be good or the same. It allows people the freedom to make mistakes and discover for themselves what is true. This same sense of freedom allows us to critically examine various views and reject them if we wish, and to communicate freely to society the reasons behind what we have decided. Criticism of religion, just as critical examination in other fields of learning like science, should also be tolerated or religious tolerance itself is not real. This is not to encourage everyone to aggressively criticize the religions of other people but to prevent the suppression of Truth under the guise of not offending anyone's religious belief.

We should acknowledge the different religions of humanity, like the different arts and sciences, taking from them what we find to be of most value, but this does not require that we don't recognize any higher or lower teachings within them or must find them to all be good. We can also have our personal preferences in religion, just as we have them in our food, clothes or job, which we don't have to all make the same.

One may prefer Hinduism, Christianity or some branch of it over other religions, but one should be willing to accept that other people may prefer their religion and yet others may not like any religion at all. One should be able to be friendly and considerate with those of different beliefs, neither having to impose one's views upon them or force such different views into a single formulation. One should be able to question the beliefs of others rationally and sincerely in one's effort to find Truth, just as others should be able to question our beliefs.

It should not be a problem for anyone if another person is a Hindu, Christian, Buddhist, Muslim, atheist or anything else. That should be the person's own right, their own affair which it is not for us individually to judge. Religion should be an individual matter, not a state or community enforced belief (which only means that it is a form of hypnosis or social control). Each individual should be free to critically examine all religious teachings and reject what they don't find to be true. Insisting that people accept the validity of all religions, just like insisting that they accept the validity of one religion, can be a form of social domination, not furthering the individual in his or her own discovery of Truth.

This is no different than how the different sects of Hinduism relate. A Shaivite and Vaishnava, for example, don't have to agree on all aspects of their beliefs to have harmony with one another. Each can think his particularly formulation of Divinity is superior. Vishnu can be made into the greatest devotee of Shiva or vice versa. We don't have to insist that we all agree with one another, which is childish, and much of the beauty of life is that we do see things differently. But we do have to learn to be considerate with those who don't agree with us. And regardless of our personal preferences we should seek to find out what is true through spiritual practices, and not merely be content with a belief or theory, which is always arbitrary.

Hinduism has always regarded freedom or liberation, Moksha, as the real goal of life. It leaves people free to discover whether the principles and views of Hinduism or Sanatana Dharma are true and does not seek to enforce them upon people, even those born as Hindus. This freedom of inquiry is the basis for real tolerance. The second factor is non-violence and its sister principle of non-interference whereby we allow others freedom to discover Truth. Through these principles all the various behavior of human beings can be brought into harmony.

True religious tolerance does not consist of reducing all religions to a single mold but of allowing the full range of human religious experience to flower without the control of any overriding dogma, hierarchy or institution in the external world. This allows us to transcend religion and does not place us under the rule of any organization. Religion is only an aid in our own Self-realization and when it becomes an end-in-itself it loses its validity. We should make human beings subject neither to one religion nor to all religions. Rather we should make religion subordinate to the Self of all creatures. We should not seek to make all religions good when religion itself is not the goal and when some religions can be harmful. We should see religions for what they are and discover the truth of what we are, in which all religions, indeed all worlds, are but our shadow.

2.5

Swami Rama Tirtha on Islam

Swami Rama Tirtha (1873-1906) was one of the greatest spiritual figures of modern India. He also visited the United States from 1902-1904 and was one of the first great Swamis to bring the Vedantic teaching to the West, following in the footsteps of Vivekananda. Though his teachings are on par with Vivekananda—indeed often more poetic and inspiring—since he formed no organization they are not as well known. Rama did not even care to collect his own writings. He was such a God-intoxicated person that the entire manifest universe did not count for anything more than straw for him. His greatness has been recognized by many great people including Mahatma Gandhi, Swami Shivananda, Paramahansa Yogananda, and Anandamayi Ma. He is lauded in yogic circles as a Jnani or man of spiritual knowledge.

Mahatma Gandhi himself said, "Swami Rama's teachings have got to be propagated. He was one of the greatest souls, not only of India but of the whole world."

Rama was a very learned man, a great poet and scholar. He knew many languages including Hindi, Urdu, English, Persian, Arabic, Sanskrit, French and German. He was not only a great Vedantin, he was also a Sufi, studied the Persian Sufi works and the Koran, which works he often quoted in his talks and writings. He spoke in Arabic to Islamic groups in Egypt during his world travels. As he was a child of the Punjab and knew the Hindu and Islamic religions intimately, his statements about Islam are worthy of note.

In 1905 he had several conversations with the Muslims in Lucknow, which has always been one of the more liberal centers of Islamic thought, largely owing to the influence of Shia Muslims, who until recently tended to be less militant and more tolerant than the main Sunni Islamic groups. These talks are recorded in the sixth volume of Rama's works, *In Woods of God Realization*. Though they are nearly a century old, they remain quite relevant today as Hindu-Muslim conflicts still prevail throughout India. The following is only a partial excerpt from these conversations which were meant to explain the validity of the Hindu religion to Indian Muslims.

Rama does not criticize or condemn Mohammed or the original teaching of Islam, though he does not equate Mohammed's realization with that of the great yogis of India either. However, he does not cover over the violence that has been done in the name of Islam, particularly in India. In the course of these conversations the word "Kafir," which is the Islamic word for infidel, came up. This is a key word for the Islamic world. A non-Muslim is called a Kafir or heretic, which is a derogatory term. The Muslims asked him his opinion on this word, as they knew of Rama's vast learning and spiritual knowledge.

Rama replied, "It would have been better if you had not put this question to Rama, because, whatever he says will be according to his own notions. Rama likes neither to flatter anybody, nor injure the feelings of anyone. Truth cannot be crushed. There is some Truth in every religion. Rama is, therefore, not only a Hindu, but also a Muslim, a Christian and a Buddhist. In answer to your question Rama will speak politely and with love, but he may also have to indulge in some plain speaking, without the least intention to injure your feelings. Rama loves you all like his own self. As such, there should be nothing to hide from his own self."

"The truth is that the followers of Islam have very wrongly interpreted the words Kufr and Kafir (the first meaning heresy and the second meaning heretic or infidel) and they have also made a very wrong use of these words. As you know, the heart of a man is the seat of God. It is a great virtue to be kind to others."

"But, unfortunately, on account of superficial knowledge or ignorance, the so-called leaders of Islam injected hatred, alienation, prejudice and violence into the hearts of ignorant Muslims, instead of preaching love for God or brotherhood of man."

"The history written by the Muslims themselves will testify and corroborate the fact that lakhs (hundreds of thousands) of non-Muslims have been butchered in whole-sale massacres, in the name of Islam. Thousands of villages were burnt to ashes by the invading Muslim armies. What brutal tyranny, intolerable harshness, absolute despotism and ruthless oppression did they not inflict on the non-Muslims in the name of Islam, due to the misinterpretation of the words, Kufr and Kafir."

"They burnt the non-Muslims alive. They did not spare even the women and the children. History says that they buried in a brick wall even the young sons of Guru Govind Singh of only eight and ten years of age, when they resolutely refused to accept Islam. They rode rough shod over all those who ever dared challenge the autocratic and dictatorial bigotry of the Muslims. With only a few noble exceptions, a very great majority of Muslims treated the non-Muslims as Kafirs (heretics). This is against the very tenets of Islam which literally means the 'Religion of peace'."

"Yet in the very name of God and His peaceful religion, Islam, His own creation has been annihilated and mercilessly cut down, under the sword of bigotry and fanaticism of ignorant Muslims. Lakhs of non-Muslims were taken prisoners and made to say goodbye to their hearths and homes, to be sold in Muslim countries as slaves to serve their masters for their whole life.

Lakhs of helpless women were made into widows. They were raped and used to satisfy the lust of the guardians of Islam. By the misuse of the words Kufr and Kafir, millions of innocent children were rendered orphans and forced to lead a life of immorality by the soldiers of Islam."

"What is all this for? Is this your Islam which you call the Religion of peace? Is terrorism the only way to make people accept Islam? This is what your own history says. This is what the world has seen of Islam. This is what the Indians have experienced. And this is what the Muslims are even today practising in India on the smallest pretext, during the communal riots, said to be engendered at the behest of our alien rulers. But no. This is not the teaching of Islam, the Religion of peace. It is due to the wrong interpretation of the words Kufr and Kafir."

"Rama has no ill will against any one of you, because he knows that the Muslim masses are misinformed and that, taking advantage of their ignorance of the Arabic language in which the holy Koran has been written, they are still being misled by their fanatic and selfish leaders."

"Rama's heart aches when he sees all this in the name of Islam and against the Farman of the Prophet who was a true and sincere devotee of God. He could not have allowed his followers unjustly and ruthlessly to butcher the innocent creation of his own God in his very name and in that of Islam, the religion which is said to establish peace on earth. But alas, after his death, not only non-Muslims but his own son-in-law, Hazrat Ali, and his (Prophet's) grandsons were mercilessly and unjustly massacred by Muslim despots, due to their vested interest, under the abominable intoxication of their false pride and prestige."

"Rama has great respect and regard for Islam. But he is extremely pained to see its fall to such a depth of degeneration that its followers, the Muslims, especially in India, have not only misused the words, Kufr and Kafir in the name of their peaceful religion, but have also indulged in all sorts of sins, murders, butchery, bloodshed, rape, hatred, jealousy, spite, prejudice, etc. against the non-Muslims, their own fellow beings and the creation of their own God or Allah."

"It is not the non-Muslims but the so-called Muslims themselves, who have defamed and vilified their own simple, veracious and unfeigned religion which is said to be preaching peace on earth. They have themselves presented an ugly image of their God-fearing and simple religion before the world."

"According to the Indian Muslims in general, Kafir is one who is not a Muslim. But this interpretation is absolutely wrong. It is for this reason that wherever they went, they, in their zeal to spread their religion, perpetrated tyranny, bloodshed and oppression. All this is against the fundamental principles of Islam, peace and total resignation to the all-pervading God."

"The person, who asserts his ego or selfishness, as against Truth is a Kafir. And what is this Truth? Truth is that which remains the same yesterday, today and forever. But Truth or Reality is only one. It is only God who is immortal, eternal, and imperishable."

"According to the Muslims, a non-Muslim is a Kafir, however God-intoxicated or truly religious-minded he may be. As such, it is said that a so-called Muslim has every right to do away with a non-Muslim, if the latter does not believe in the Prophet Mohammed, or in the Koran, as if he, the non-Muslim, has not been created by the same God. It is also said that a Muslim will be forgiven by God for his sins just because he is a formal Muslim. This is a popular belief among the Muslim masses. All this misbelief or blind faith is against the fundamental principles of Islam. From the point of view of Rama, cruelty due to narrow-mindedness, does not become those who profess that Islam is the religion of peace."

"It is now for you to say, how reasonable, just and fair it is to preach to the ignorant Muslim masses, segregation in the name of Islam, which is obviously for political reasons with vested interests. The entire universe is one due to direct connection with God, the universal creator. If your own God has made people take birth into non-Muslim families, who are you to shed their blood, annihilate them or hate them after taking them to be Kafirs? How do you justify yourself in finding fault with God's doing? How dare you interfere with his planning."

"Oh dear friends, according to your own Koran, all are equal in the eyes of God who is the Rabbul-Almin, the Lord of all the worlds. We all emanate from Him. We all are His sons. Will God be ever pleased with you to see His sons being massacred by you in His very name? No father can be happy to see this cruelty of yours. Who are you, then, to create differences and disunity in the so-called Kafirs and the Muslims, when God is common to all? Please reflect and say honestly, if you yourself are a real Muslim? Are you not a Kafir yourself, when you deny God, by acting practically all the time with selfish motives? This is certainly not the teaching of Islam, the religion of peace."

"Rama regrets very much to have to say all this. But since Rama has great respect and regard for Islam, due to its simplicity and direct faith in God and, since he takes the Muslims as his own self, he does not feel any hesitation in speaking frankly and fearlessly to his own self. Rama says with love and good intentions only what he thinks to be right from his own experience and observation, because it is sin to hide anything from his own dear ones. If he is wrong he may be corrected, Rama will not have the least objection to this."

Swami Ram Tirtha does not criticize Islam, nor its prophet nor its book. In this he follows in the wake of other Hindu religious teachers and thinkers. What is exceptional about him is that he knows so much about Islamic history and speaks about it with such frankness, exercising no *negationism* about it. And that is the most significant part of this essay. His knowledge of Islamic history does not however make him change his views of Islam as a religion. He thinks that all that the best of Muslim heroes did and Muslim teachers taught was "against the fundamental principles of Islam." And in this way, he is able to retain his "respect and regard for Islam." In this respect too he follows in the wake of other Hindu savants and students of Islam who think they know Islam better than the best of Muslim theologians, and cannot resist the temptation of speaking "not only as a Hindu, but also as a Muslim and as a Christian."

But if a truthful account of Indian history is made, we need not accuse those who give such accounts as being prejudiced against Muslims because such history does not show Islam in a positive light. If we do we will have to throw the likes of Swami Rama Tirtha into such a category.

Rama also stated to the Indians: "Please study your own history with care and attention, you will please mark that, so long as we were strictly following the basic tenets of our Sanatana Dharma, which is based on mutual love, unity and selfless discharge of our moral duty, with faith in God, no outside power could dare look at us with evil designs." Hindus today need to look at their history in that light of dharma. Only then will emerge the true way to develop the country for the future.

2.6

A Comment on Ram Swarup's *Hindu View of Christianity and Islam*

There are many books available in the world today that provide critiques of different religions from both religious and non-religious standpoints. Most religions have their own books stating their position relative to the others and pointing out the unique validity of their faith. Strangely, however, it is difficult to find any real Hindu critique of predominant Western religions, though much criticism of Hinduism, generally inaccurate, is easy to discover from their point of view. However, now there is at least one important Hindu critique of Western religions, Ram Swarup's *Hindu View of Christianity and Islam,* which examines these religions from the standpoint of yogic spirituality and points out the difference between religion as an internal quest in the Eastern world and religion as an external conversion oriented social movement in the West.

There are several reasons for the lack of books explaining the Hindu point of view on different religions. In the Western world authentic accounts of Hinduism are difficult to get. The literature generally comes from two sources. The first is a rather dry academic Western scholarship on Hinduism, coming from non-Hindus or even people who have no real sympathy for the religion. These scholars are largely either Christian theologians or Marxists in their views. They represent a critique of Hinduism from a non-Hindu point of view, though ironically their books are looked to by those seeking to find out what Hinduism is. The second source is the work of various Swamis and Gurus who have come to the West. Their groups largely promote the particular approach of their teacher and, with a few notable exceptions, seldom examine Hinduism (Sanatana Dharma) as a whole. Hence there are many books in the West on Yoga, particularly asanas, various works on meditation, or general books of wisdom by teachers from India, but it is difficult to find any real explication of Hinduism within them.

In India there is a reluctance to provide a Hindu critique of other religions but for different reasons. India as a Hindu majority country has a policy of not offending minorities in matters of religion. As India's minorities are Christian and Islamic little critical is allowed of these religions not merely by the government but by anyone. Even an accurate account of how these groups have functioned historically in India, which has included persecution or, in the case of Islam, genocide, has been suppressed in the name of communal harmony. Ram Swarup has challenged this attitude of suppressing Truth for political reasons, and examined the actual teachings and historical record of these religions for good or ill.

This reluctance to allow Hindus in India their perspective on other religions is also rather strange because in Christian or Islamic countries, Hinduism, if it is tolerated at all, is generally explained in a very negative manner as a religion of strange cults, idol worship, widow burning, and dowry deaths. I am speaking as a writer on Hinduism in the United States and have to frequently deal with these negative stereotypes. Even in academic circles in this country there is a reluctance to accept that Hinduism is a religion at all but merely a collection of cults. One university here recently published the view of a prominent American professor of Asian Studies that Hinduism is a modern political expropriation of various unrelated cults for nationalist ambitions and that prior to the last century there was no such thing as Hinduism in India, and no such thing as India as a country!

More liberally religious minded people in the West are not informed about the situation in India and Asia. They don't realize that the fundamentalist groups which they often criticize or even ridicule in America are engaged in massive conversion efforts in India, openly spreading various distortions about such religions as Hinduism and Buddhism in their own countries with little being done to counter them. Most people in the West think that the days of missionary activity ended with the colonial era. The result is that people in the West are remarkably misinformed about Hinduism, even those who may be practicing some Hindu based Yoga or meditation approaches. Few people in the West can give an accurate idea of what Hinduism is. And many people in the West, even those who may be sympathetic, are inclined to accept distorted views of Hinduism because they do not find any other point of view presented.

A Hindu critique of Western religions, such as Ram Swarup provides in his book, is therefore essential to provide a balanced view on the subject. The main modern Hindu critique of other religions that can be found today is not a critique at all but a statement that all religions are good, that all are the same, their beliefs and practices are equal, and if they merely respected one another then all would be well in the world. Non-Hindu groups regard this as a form of emotionalism or confused thinking, and would never equate their religions with Hinduism and its guru or deity cults. Hindus under this view may never study other religions and find out what their teachings really say, which in many cases is very different than what Hinduism teaches. This synthetic Hindu view thereby often serves only to inhibit any deep inquiry or profound study.

All religions are not merely the same and equally good, as

Ram Swarup points out. All water is also one but not all water is fit to drink. Though all water is one we must still be careful with the particular water that we actually drink. Ramakrishna, one of the Hindu saints who is looked to for this all religions are the same doctrine, practiced Islam for three days and in a highly unorthodox manner, visualized Christ but never really practiced Christianity, while practicing various Hindu teachings on a daily basis for over thirty years. His point was not that all religions are the same and equal ways to Self-realization, which is not even true of all the branches of Hinduism, but that there is something good in all religions, just as there is in all people.

Nor do the other religions simply say what Hinduism states but with different words. Hinduism has its metaphysics of karma and rebirth, which is quite unlike the heaven-hell doctrines of Christianity and Islam. Hinduism views liberation, Self-realization or communion with God as the highest goal, not merely salvation from sin which is the Christian view. Hinduism emphasizes spiritual experience, gained through self-discipline, Yoga and meditation. It does not look to prayer, good works or conversion of others as the answer to the human problem, or mere belief in a particular religion and its dogma as being capable of changing our consciousness. While it is true that there have been Christian and Islamic mystics who have views or practices akin to the Hindu and engaged in the inner quest, these individuals have been exceptions, were generally persecuted and rejected, and represent very little of what goes on in the name of these religions today.

I will give an example of the distortion caused by this Hindu view that all religions are the same. Talking before a group of people in Delhi during a visit to India last year I spoke of the difference between karma and rebirth oriented religions like Hinduism and Buddhism and those like Christianity and Islam which teach that we have only one life. A Hindu in the audience objected and said that the Bible also teaches karma and rebirth under the statement "as you sow so shall you reap." I told the person that this was his Hindu interpretation of the Bible and that almost every single Christian church of every denomination in the United States would throw him out if he tried to teach such things to their congregations. He was shocked to find this out.

Hinduism begins with the statement from its oldest Rig Veda "that which is the One Truth, the sages call by many different names." This is quite a different statement then "There is no God but Allah, and Mohammed is his final prophet," or "Jesus is the only Son of God," which the great majority of Muslims and Christians believe. For this reason Hinduism has maintained a broad and comprehensive spiritual approach and has not become a proselytizing ideology. While Hinduism states that there is good in all religions as in all people, this does not mean that it has no conscience that the rest of the world needs to hear. Its critique of missionary movements, materialist ideologies (including communism), its defense of indigenous peoples and their cultures, its defense of the Earth and of animals, provides Hinduism a crucial voice today when our planet is being overrun by economic and ideological interests which are threatening its very life. Ram Swarup has found this Hindu conscience and is willing to proclaim it to the world, which is sadly in need of its message.

Ram Swarup is perhaps the foremost living thinker in the field of Hinduism. He is leading the most significant and thorough Hindu examination of Western religions to date. He presents a logical and profound critique of Christianity and Islam showing their shortcomings from the standpoint of Hindu spirituality. He clearly discriminates between yogic spirituality which is the essence of Eastern Dharmic traditions and exclusive belief systems such as Christianity and Islam have presented themselves. His chapter on Semitic Religions and Yogic Spirituality is a classic in this regard. His views are always clear, compassionate but straightforward, not hiding the facts but revealing the Truth for the benefit of all.

Ram Swarup copiously quotes from Christian and Islamic sources. Much of what he has done is merely presenting what these religions have said about themselves, so that those who have interpreted these religions from a Hindu point of view can see how such groups actually see themselves. His work is not a mere traditional Hindu reaction against the West or the modern world. Ram Swarup has a global and futuristic vision that is examining the spiritual problems of humanity, which Hinduism offers an important, if not crucial, perspective on.

Unfortunately there has been a call by minority interests in India to ban Ram Swarup's book, the same group that has brought about the banning of a number of books in the country like Salman Rushdie's *Satanic Verses*. While it is alright for non-Hindu religions to criticize Hinduism, it appears that it is not right for Hindus to express their own point of view, even in India. If it is not acceptable for Hinduism in India to defend itself in the current information (or disinformation) war, where is it to be given a voice?

The banning of books is the greatest statement of both intolerance and stupidity. A country which does this is just giving a lobotomy to itself. In the Western world there is a freedom of speech. No books are banned. One can find numerous books criticizing Christianity and Jesus, for example, including some by great Western thinkers like Voltaire and Nietzsche. Both the Bible and the Koran themselves contain much criticism of Pagan religions and their cultures. Why can't Pagan religions give their critique of the religions which have been attacking them for centuries? It is the sign of a mature culture that it can accept criticism and tolerate various points of view. We don't all see things the same way and intelligence grows through the examination of different points of view, not through insisting that one point of view alone is true. A culture that has to pass laws banning books or anti-blasphemy laws preventing a particular religious group from being criticized (but usually accepting or encouraging the denigration of other religious groups), is an immature culture. To appease those who require books banned is only to appease this form of immaturity, which destroys intelligence.

Traditional Hindu books contain much dialogue, questioning, discussion and various critiques. The Hindu and Buddhist philosophical traditions have a lively tradition of debate, critiquing not only different religions but different branches of their same religion. In Vedantic books, like those of Shankaracarya, there are critiques of other systems of Hinduism like Sankhya and the different Buddhist systems like Vijnanavada or Madhyamika. In Buddhist philosophical works there are critiques of different branches of Buddhism and other Hindu systems like Sankhya and Vedanta. Such religious thinkers did not have the idea that it was good not to have any critique of different systems, as someone might get offended in the process of having their views questioned. There was an open pursuit of Truth and everything was to be questioned.

The same thing is true in science today. While there is only one science this does not mean that all scientists are good, that all scientific theories are correct, or that minority scientists should be given special treatment as regards their theories, which non-minorities should not be allowed to question. Such thinking does not lead us to Truth but confuses free intellectual inquiry with political concerns and vote banks.

India needs to get out of the intellectual morass it has gotten itself into through such intellectual appeasement. Ram Swarup shows how to reverse this process. How his books are accepted is a good measure of how India is willing to honesty deal with its conscience. Hinduism is a voice of Truth that needs to be shared with all of humanity. Apologists of Hinduism and Hindu appeasers of non-Hindus have missed the spiritual essence of the tradition, which is that Truth is greater than all beliefs, authorities, books and institutions.

2.7
Yogic Spirituality and Islam

A number of those who proclaim that all religions are one like to carry this principle further and make the founders of all religions into Divine incarnations (avatars). They would equate such figures as Krishna, Buddha, Christ, Mohammed, and Moses as if there were no fundamental difference between them and their teachings. Such people are generally influenced by yogic spirituality that perceives a unity of Truth behind all religions and regards religion as a means to Self-realization or union with God.

They would see a common yogic spiritual experience behind all religions and proclaim that the founders of all important religious movements were great yogis and Self-realized sages, as if that were the only model of religion possible. They may lump together belief-oriented religions—like Christianity and Islam—along with meditation traditions—like Hinduism and Buddhism—which can be very different, and leave out religious traditions that have no organized approach like Native American and African traditions. To explain the evident differences between yogic spirituality and other religions, they propose that the teachings of the founders of the religions—like Christ or Mohammed—were misinterpreted and that what was originally a path to God-realization based on a yogic model in time became reduced to a dogma, church or ritual by followers who lost track of the internal dimension of the teaching. They would claim the same for Hinduism to explain the difference between its yogic and ritualistic approaches.

There are clearly common factors between all religions, particularly ethical principles of leading a good life, though there are differences on this level as well. The religious or mystical experience has yet more similarities, though it is not all of the same type either, as the different levels and stages of spiritual growth reveal. Above all, there is only One Truth that all spiritual aspiration is moving toward. But this does not mean that all religions have understood this Truth in the same manner or to the same degree, or that their founders must have done so. While it may be better to emphasize the similarities between religions than the differences, when we overly exaggerate their similarities, we create a misunderstanding of another order that also does not serve the purpose of discovering the Truth. We may give everyone the impression that their religion, whatever it is, is sufficient, when for the full flowering of the spiritual life it may be necessary for them to go beyond it.

The point of this article is that some of the religions of the world and their founders—and one in particular, Islam and Mohammed, which is perhaps the most evident example—do not follow the model of yogic spirituality, if we really look at what they have to say about themselves. They reflect a very different view of religion. To try to turn all religions, and all forms of mysticism, into versions of yogic spirituality is not intellectually accurate, nor is it sensitive to what these religions themselves say, nor is it based on a real study of them. On the contrary, it usually represents the view of those who have not really looked into what non-yogic religions are all about. Those trained in the unity tradition are inclined to read a yogic type spirituality between the lines of all religious teachings, even though the great majority of those who follow these religions—including their leaders and mystics who have arisen within them—may not accept important yogic principles and practices as valid.

There are obviously other models of religion than yogic spirituality as the various religious teachings in the world clearly reveal. Many religious groups do not emphasize a yogic type purity of body and mind, nor do they teach yogic-like meditational practices, or have a yogic goal like liberation from rebirth and realization of unity with God. They may not look to non-violent or meditative figures as their guides but to people of active or militant dispositions. They may not emphasize an internal yogic-like quest but promote external actions, even war to spread their faith. As this is the case, there is no reason to insist that at least some of the founders of different religions could not have had the same views as their proponents today.

Whether the yogic model of spirituality is not the only approach, is not entirely valid, or whether some religions are deficient depends upon if one considers the principles of yogic spirituality to be universal. But to pretend that all religions derive, at least originally, from a model of yogic spirituality and therefore are all equally true and must lead to the same goal, though they may not recognize it as their aim, cannot stand scrutiny. It is neither fair to yogic spirituality or to other religions to assume they are simply the same thing in a different guise or misinterpreted.

Mohammed According to Vivekananda

As the founder of one of the world's predominant religions, Mohammed is regarded by some following this ecumenical view as a Divine incarnation, great yogi, or Self-realized sage. Most people who make this judgement have not studied the life of Mohammed or understood the Islamic view of Mohammed, which does not view him in this light. They merely assume it is the case because Islam is a widely believed religion or because various mystics, like the Sufis, have arisen in the course of its history.

As a holy book or scripture, such people may regard the Koran as the Word of God—like the Bible or the Gita or other so-called scriptures—and may say that they believe in the Koran and consider that it has the same teaching as other scriptures. Again such people usually have not studied the Koran and may not really believe in or follow much of what it actually says. Nor are they giving credence to traditional Islamic interpretations of the Koran.

Who was Mohammed? Swami Vivekananda, who is often regarded as one of the main figures behind this new ecumenicalism, critiqued Mohammed from the standpoint of yogic spirituality. According to him Mohammed was a man who stumbled upon a spiritual experience without the proper training. To quote the Swami from his book on Raja Yoga:

"The Yogi says there is a great danger in stumbling upon this state. In a good many cases there is the danger of the brain being deranged, and, as a rule, you will find that all those men, however great they were, who stumbled upon this superconscious state without understanding it, groped in the dark, and generally had, along with their knowledge, some quaint superstitions. They opened themselves to hallucinations. Mohammed claimed that the Angel Gabriel came to him in a cave one day and took him on the heavenly horse, Harak, and he visited the heavens. But with all that, Mohammed spoke some most wonderful truths mixed with superstitions. How will you explain it? That man was inspired, no doubt, but was not a trained Yogi, and did not know the reason of what he was doing. Think of the good Mohammed did to the world, and think of the great evil that has been done through his teachings, mothers bereft of their children, children made orphans, whole countries destroyed, millions upon millions of people killed."

According to Vivekananda, Mohammed, like many untrained people in the spiritual life, upon having a spiritual experience jumped to the conclusion that he had the Word of God, and that the world should follow the religion God had revealed to him. Whether one agrees with Vivekananda or not, he is simply applying the principles of yogic spirituality to the commonly known life and teachings of Mohammed, thinking that these yogic principles are universally valid.

The idea of a final prophet, such as Mohammed is claimed to be, is contrary to the idea of yogic spirituality that spiritual knowledge is a human capacity, like art, science, or mechanical skills, albeit of a higher nature. As a capacity of all human beings, it cannot exclusively or finally belong to any one person. There cannot be any final painter, for example, beyond whom no real painters can ever be born, or any final scientist, beyond whom no important new scientific discoveries can be made. Any insistence upon a final or exclusive revelation of God for a certain person is contrary to the universality of the yogic view.

The Life and Teaching of Mohammed

If we examine his life from Islamic traditional sources we see that Mohammed did not follow a number of yogic principles in his daily life. Nor was he taught yogic practices like mantra, pranayama or meditation by a living master trained in such a tradition, though he did come into contact with various religious influences in the caravan world around him. He did not experience a situation like that found among the Himalayan yogis or in the great temples and monasteries of the Hindus and Buddhists where a complete yogic type training could be gained.

Mohammed knew little or nothing about Hinduism or Buddhism and their approaches, which he does not mention, and used the Biblical model to represent spirituality as a whole. Mohammed came into contact with a number of Jews and Christians, and with the Bible through them. His teaching was most influenced by the Old Testament and he appears to have styled himself after the Old Testament prophets and their struggles against the Pagan Philistines and Canaanites, in whose image his enemies and non-Muslims in general were portrayed, curiously including the Jews themselves. While Christ reformed the Old Testament Law of an eye for an eye and a tooth for a tooth and instituted the idea of turning one's cheek—a concept of non-violence that may have come from a yogic influence—Mohammed reintroduced the harsher law of the earlier era.

Mohammed began to receive his revelations after the late age of forty, before which he lived a fairly ordinary life. His revelations appeared as a trance that he went into periodically. He accepted these experiences as a direct communion with God that no other human being could have. He claimed to talk with the angel Gabriel and with God (Allah) himself, who he states appointed him as His final Prophet. Mohammed spoke of the Koran as the Word of God, given to him for all humanity for the rest of history until the Day of the Final Judgement.

Mohammed always referred to himself as the Prophet and servant of God. At his death he spoke of going to Heaven, not of merging into the formless Divine. Mohammed does not speak of the Self or Atman or make statements like "I am God (*aham Brahmo'smi*)," the hallmark of Self-realized sages. According to orthodox Islam no individual should proclaim "I am God," which is a delusion. God and the individual are different and the individual should never arrogate realization of God to himself. For saying this the ninth century Sufi Al-Hallaj was cut into pieces and thrown into a river by other Muslims. The reason is because Mohammed, the greatest and final Prophet, did not say this and for a Muslim to claim even what Mohammed did not, would be blasphemy of the greatest order.

Mohammed does speak of various mystical experiences, including communication with spirits, fighting with devils, and the descent of Divine grace and power. He speaks of effacement into Allah, but God or Allah as the Creator is the supreme term. There is neither Atman, the Self, nor Brahman, the formless Absolute, nor does he mention the law of karma or the cycle of rebirth and the need to transcend it. Mohammed appears to have been a dualist, or one who thinks that God and the soul are different, though related, and he does not speak of non-duality. Orthodox Islam follows a dualistic philosophy based on his example.

Mohammed's God was beyond all images and commanded Mohammed to convert or conquer those who use images and icons (idols) in their worship. Yet it is wrong to consider that Mohammed's Allah is the same as the Absolute of Vedantic thought. Mohammed's God possesses emotions like anger and jealousy. He talks to his chosen people and his special Prophet and directs them to specific actions that may involve violence against people of other beliefs. His God is concerned with political events and aids Mohammed in various personal struggles and military battles. Allah has prepared heaven for those who believe in Him and hell for those who don't. He is not a detached Transcendent Reality like the Brahman of Vedanta or the Dharmakaya of Buddhism, though He places Himself beyond all representation.

It is clear therefore that Mohammed does not represent the state of God-consciousness from birth that Divine incarnations (avatars) are supposed to have from the standpoint of yogic spirituality. Nor does he show an ongoing state of Samadhi in the yogic sense beginning at any time in his life, which is experienced as an unbroken continuity of awareness of the Supreme Self. He had mystical experiences but these came at various intervals. Not surprisingly therefore orthodox Islam does not believe in avatars or Self-realization, as Mohammed, their greatest Prophet, does not reflect such awareness.

Nor are prophethood and avatarhood the same thing as religious syncretists would have us believe. A prophet has a special message from God that is said to be valid for all people and which establishes an external code of belief that everyone is supposed to follow. An avatar is one whose consciousness from birth is that of the Divine Itself and sets forth a path of Self-realization based on yogic practices. Islam does not accept Divine incarnations and this is one important difference it has always had with Christianity. It does not accept the Christian concept of Jesus as the Son of God but only as a previous prophet. To try to make Mohammed into an avatar in the Hindu sense shows neither an understanding of what a prophet or an avatar is.

The Character of Mohammed and Yogic Principles

Mohammed was a pious and disciplined person, had a high standard of cleanliness, and gave up drinking alcohol. He readily took poor people and slaves, including blacks, into his congregation and was very loving and broad-minded with his followers. He regarded all of his followers like members of his own family, as one great brotherhood, and was not attached to race, class or learning. He never accumulated money or possessions for himself, even when they were freely available. He did not build expensive mosques but preferred simple dwellings and plain places of worship. He did not try to create a priestly order to rule over people and mediate between them and God but tried to create a religion in which each person could communicate to God directly through prayer. He spent his life working tirelessly according to the dictates of his mission. Yet Mohammed demonstrated at least two significant traits that are incompatible with the idea of him as a sage in the yogic sense.

First he was prone to violence with those who criticized Allah, Mohammed's role as the Prophet, or Mohammed's followers. He saw the value of promoting his religion by force, if necessary, during the more than eighty battles that he fought. After his exile from Mecca, Mohammed organized numerous raids on caravans to Mecca. He fought as the leader of his army, in both offensive and defensive conflicts, and was once severely wounded. He took and ransomed hostages. He had a group of seven hundred Jews of the Banu Quraiza tribe massacred after they surrendered to him and became his prisoners, when he determined that he could not trust them. He at times approved of his followers performing assassinations to eliminate enemies of the faith (for example Asma, a woman poet of Mecca, who was killed by Omeir, one of Mohammed's followers for criticizing Mohammed). He even burned down the date orchards of his enemies, not even sparing the trees. This is at least what traditional Islamic records of him relate.

Mohammed is credited with introducing Islamic law codes, which like most medieval law codes contain much that the modern world regards as unnecessary cruelty, including cutting off of the hands and feet of criminals for certain offenses. Orthodox Muslims today say that Islamic law cannot be changed because to do so would be to alter what the Prophet has said. We do not see in Mohammed the practice of non-violence emphasized in Yoga traditions or found in the life of Christ. Mohammed forgave all those who embraced Islam and tried hard to promote non-violence among Muslims but his record with non-Muslims was quite different. No doubt some of the violence found in the life of Mohammed was part of his time and culture. Mohammed was often oppressed and attacked, but the higher degree of compassion for all people—regardless of their beliefs—cannot be attributed to him.

According to the Sufis, Mohammed emphasized that there was an inner holy war and an outer holy war, the former being work on oneself and the latter being fighting for the religion, and that the inner holy war was more important. Yet he never gave up the need for the outer holy war, which became a war of world conquest for his successors according to the intention Mohammed himself set forth to spread his faith to the Greek and Persian empires and conquer them if necessary.

Mohammed's second character trait that is not part of the yogic spiritual approach was his approach to sexuality. Mohammed at twenty-five married a woman of forty and was married to her until her death twenty-five years later. He was a good husband (though not a yogi who had transcended sexual desire). After the age of fifty, when his first wife had passed away, Mohammed in time married eight additional women who were generally young and beautiful. He married Aisha, the daughter of his friend and companion Abu Bakr, when she was six and consummated the marriage when she was nine. In other words he married and had conjugal relations with a minor, though he himself was an elderly man. Another one of his marriages that appears quite unusual was that to a woman named Zainab, who was originally the wife of his adopted son Zaid, who divorced her to allow Mohammed to marry her, and then ceased calling himself the son of Mohammed.

Brahmacharya or transcendence of the sexual urge is thus not represented in the life of the prophet. Not surprisingly, Islam forbids monasticism and is against celibacy, and in its holy wars Islamic militants have at times marked out monks and monasteries for destruction, regarding them as unholy. Mohammed did give each of his wives her own house and stayed with each on alternate days, engaging in regular sexual relations with them up to the time of his death, and appears to have treated all his wives kindly. He made Islam forbid sex outside of marriage, particularly premarital sex, though it does allow a man to have up to four wives.

Following Mohammed, Islam promotes the having of children as part of one's religious duty and as part of its strategy to spread itself in the world. It does not accept the renunciate-ascetic view as found in the life of the Buddha, and such as colors even the householder life in India. It therefore does not have the respect for monks, swamis and yogis that goes along with such a view.

Mohammed's Companions

If we look at Mohammed's companions and successors we

see men who had similar life-styles as Mohammed, though like Mohammed they may have been mystics and were pious in their religious beliefs. They do not include monks or yogis, or people who talked of or sought Self-realization, but became generals who led armies trying to conquer the world, something we cannot imagine any yogi attempting to do. The first Caliph Abu Bakr was a merchant turned general. Like Mohammed he and the successive Caliphs (heads of Islam) were simultaneously the leader of the army, the political leader and chief judge, as well as the leader of the religion. In addition Islamic generals and soldiers, starting with Mohammed's successors, took personally from the wealth of the lands they conquered and set up hereditary pensions for themselves and their families. They turned themselves not into ascetics but into the new ruling class.

Some Muslims, particularly members of the Shia branch, claim that Mohammed was not militaristic, but that the Caliphs, starting with Abu Bakr, misinterpreted his teaching—that what was a defensive struggle in the life of Mohammed trying to preserve Islam in the face of unfair attack, became an offensive battle after he died, an attempt to promote their version of Islam through force. In time conflict arose among the followers of Mohammed, between the party of Ali, his son-in-law, and the party of the Caliphs. Ali and his sons, the grandsons of Mohammed, were killed in battle with other Muslims and with them Mohammed's blood line perished. Ali is regarded by the Shias and some Sufis as the true representative of Mohammed's teaching who was not tainted by the violence and luxury that the Caliphs assumed.

However, in support of the Sunni view (those who accept the Caliphs), we should note that all three early Caliphs—Abu Bakr, Omar and Othman, whom the Shias do not accept and who promoted the Islamic invasion and conquest of Africa and the Middle East—were among the closest living disciples of Mohammed. Mohammed took daughters of the first two among his wives and married two of his daughters to the third. If anyone would have known Mohammed and been in a position to continue his work, it would have been them. The Caliphs were not like Saint Paul of Christianity, who never knew Christ personally, but the direct disciples of the Prophet. What they did, they felt, through their own experience of the Prophet, was fulfilling his will.

Mohammed and the Koran

If we examine the life of Mohammed it could be argued that we do see a great man in a number of ways. But we cannot regard Mohammed as a yogi or avatar in the traditional Hindu or Buddhist sense unless we are willing to rewrite the facts of his life and teaching. Even most Muslims would not portray him in this light. Mohammed was a poet, mystic, religious reformer, political leader and victorious general, but he did not follow the life of a yogi or give his teachings in harmony with the yogic approach, nor did he have the behavior of what Christians would call a saint.

The Koran, one could similarly argue, is a great book with much poetry, mysticism, history and theology, but not the Word of God or Absolute Truth. If it is the Word of God that God is very different than the Divine Reality of yogic traditions, who is not a personal God involved in the affairs of the world, like Allah. The Koran cannot honestly be said to be a yogic teaching like the Bhagavad Gita, for example, and does not speak of meditation, karma or liberation. Not surprisingly, Muslims see in the Koran a very different view of the Divine than in yogic texts like the Gita.

A case for religious tolerance is made in the Koranic statement that there should be no compulsion in religion. This statement of non-compulsion merely means that in religion we (Muslims) will go our way and those who don't agree with us can go their way, which way we do not approve of. This we will go our way and you can go your's is not a statement of mutual sympathy or respect. It is the potentially hostile tolerance of those who have different views but are unable to change one another. Many Islamic thinkers consider that this statement of tolerance is abrogated by the verse on Jihad which encourages Muslims to actively strive to convert non-Muslims, using force if necessary.

We find in the Koran no such statement that all religions are true—that Christianity, Judaism, Zoroastrianism, and the indigenous religions of Arabia are as good as or equal to Islam. All other religions and their followers are frequently criticized. According to the Koran, whatever value they may have had has ceased with Islam, which is meant to replace them.

We should note that orthodox Muslims regard such non-yogic traits of Mohammed as laudable. Nor do they see they see the necessity for yogic practices, since Mohammed himself did not do them. They do not dispute these facts but interpret them differently. They regard non-violence as a character weakness or lack of conviction and are proud of the conquests that Islam has made in its invasion of other countries. Orthodox Muslims see Islam as a superior path to yogic teachings because it can lead a person to God without requiring such disciplines as the yogic which, after all, very few people are able to really do. They regard Islam as a direct connection to God, which takes one beyond the need to perform yogic practices, should these be of any value at all. Yet the connection with God they seek is going to heaven or paradise, much like the Christians. It is not the Nirvana or liberation from the cycle of birth and death of yogic paths, which orthodox Muslims would regard as a delusion.

Sufism, Orthodox Islam, and Yoga

As there has been a notable Sufi mystical tradition in Islam, a number of people have used this to regard Mohammed as an illumined sage. Sufis like Rumi appear to have been great mystics, if not God-realized sages on par with the great yogis, and some would assume that Mohammed, whom most Sufis revere, must have been of the same understanding. This view is enhanced by the fact that today, particularly in the West or in India, there are Sufis who proclaim the unity of all religions, and some who believe in karma and rebirth, practice vegetarianism, and otherwise appear more as part of the yogic tradition than what most people, including Muslims, would consider to be representative of Islam.

This view assumes two points that are questionable, even by Muslims. The first is that a Sufi-type mysticism was represented by Mohammed himself. The second is that Sufi mysticism is of the same nature as yogic traditions. Most Muslims do not accept that Mohammed, or Islam based upon him, is in harmony with Sufism. In fact, orthodox Islam generally opposes the Sufis. They accept that Mohammed had experience of God as His Prophet, but consider that it is heresy and arrogance for others to attempt to gain such experiences. They often regard the Sufis not as true Muslims but as proponents of pre- or non-Islamic, and therefore heretical traditions like Vedanta.

Sufis have been frequently attacked or even massacred under Islamic regimes from Morocco to India, including in this century. Sufis are oppressed in fundamentalist Islamic countries today and are in danger of losing their lives should they openly proclaim what they are doing. Sufism is illegal in Saudi Arabia, and if there are any in Iran, they are in hiding. Even in India the Sufis were sometimes killed by Islamic rulers. Aurangzeb, the fundamentalist Islamic Moghul ruler of the seventeenth century included among those he killed his own brother Dara, who was a Sufi, and the Sufi Sarmad, who sought peace with the Hindus and honored yogic spirituality.

Moreover, there are two main groups of Sufis, who are a highly complex phenomenon containing many different points of view. We should note that the term Sufi can stand for intellectuals, artists, occultists, and mystics in Islamic society whether orthodox or unorthodox and sometimes even is used as a family name.

One group of Sufis, who could be called "liberal Sufis," are rebels from orthodox Islam, and often look for the origins of their teachings in earlier Christian and Persian mysticism or in Hinduism and Buddhism, criticizing orthodox Islam. The other and more numerous group of Sufis, who could be called "orthodox Sufis," speaks highly of Mohammed and the secrets of the Koran and appears as orthodox Muslims, accepting the Sharia or traditional Islamic law. While liberal Sufis share their spiritual teachings with members of other religions and do not actively promote conversion, orthodox Sufis require that people first become orthodox Muslims before receiving Sufis teachings and work strongly at converting people to Islam.

The liberal Sufis are more in harmony with the yogic tradition and at times have had a common cause with it against militant and anti-mystical Islam. The yogic tradition has had much sympathy for these Sufis and has always tried to help them. This group is more common among Sufis in India and in the West (though it appears to be in the minority everywhere), who are generally not so grounded in orthodox Islam, and also among the Shias who are the main Islamic sect in Persia (which retained much of its pre-Islamic culture). Most of the great mystical Sufis belong to this line. Such Sufis are promoted as models of tolerance but it would be wrong to attribute their tolerance to Islam, which is rarely tolerant. Their tolerance derives more from pre-Islamic traditions, and in the case of Indian Sufis derives from their Hindu roots (particularly Indian Sufis who follow Hindu musical and related mystical traditions).

The orthodox Sufis seldom accept yogic teachings and disciplines, though they may be mystics. They generally support militant Islam and may be among its leading proponents (even if this requires disguising the fact that they are Sufis in order not to offend the orthodox). This group is more common in traditional

Islamic regions like Africa and the Near East, though it appears predominant everywhere, even in India, and has often supplanted the more liberal Sufis. It relates primarily to the Sunni branch of Islam, which is the majority Islamic sect everywhere except Iran, including India, Central Asia and Indonesia.

In the West these two lines of Sufis may criticize each other. Liberal Sufis, who may use teachings from all religions, regard the orthodox Sufis as narrow minded. Orthodox Sufis may style themselves "Islamic Sufis" to distinguish themselves from liberal Sufis, whom they regard as unorthodox and impure for mixing other religions with Islam in their Sufism. Such Islamic Sufis see themselves as the spiritual power behind Islam and are promoting the Islamization of the world. However it is not always possible to distinguish between these two groups of Sufis, who may be mixed together in various ways.

Sometimes orthodox Sufis appear as liberal Sufis in non-Islamic countries, promoting harmony and communication between spiritual traditions, which allows them to gain a foothold. Once established they reveal their more orthodox nature by their support of the Sharia, burka (veiling of women), and their attempt to convert people to Islam. Some Sufi groups coming into the West today have employed this strategy.

The more orthodox Sufis participated in holy wars and led military expeditions in India, Central Asia and Europe. They were not universally mystics, nor was their mysticism always of a non-violent variety. They used force to promote Islam, which they perpetrated against the yogis and monks of India. Many Sufis today have the same opinions. As one Turkish Sufi who spoke recently in America remarked, "Islam has no place for pacifist vegetarians. Mohammed fought wars and ate meat."

Even famous medieval Persian Sufi poets like Attar, Omar Khayyam (for example, *Rubaiyat* 44) and Sanai, in their poems praised the Afghan King Mahmud of Ghazni as the ideal king and Islamic ruler for defeating the dark infidels and smashing their idols. These dark infidels were the Hindus and their great idol was the magnificent Somnath Shiva temple in Gujarat, one of their most sacred sites, which Mahmud plundered as part of his devastation of the country and massacre of thousands of Hindus. Islamic writers saw Mahmud as a second Mohammed for his victory over the infidels and smashing their temples. To such Sufi poets, Mahmud was only another example of a pious Muslim destroying idolaters, such as the Koran approved. While perhaps they didn't know the real barbarism of what Mahmud did, they don't seem to have questioned such activity. Few Sufis appear to have made any real efforts to stop the Islamic invasions in India or elsewhere, even though orthodox Islamic kings sometimes targeted them along with the infidels. Sufi poets usually glorified the Islamic conquests of Hindu and Buddhist lands and did not see much value in their pre-Islamic cultures.

Hence it is wrong to interpret all Sufi mysticism as another version of the yogic model, though liberal Sufi groups can appear in this light, and a few Sufis can be placed on par with the great yogis. Most Sufis do not accept karma and rebirth as true. Most don't ascribe to several of the ethical principles of yogic approaches (particularly non-violence or monastic vows), though they may perform meditation or devotional practices. Sufis who recognize that one can find God through yogic paths may regard such yogic disciplines as complicated and indirect—only necessary because one is unwilling to take the direct route of Islam, the surrender to Allah that Mohammed taught—which they claim can lead even ordinary people to spiritual realization without the need of yogic methods or disciplines. This at least is what one Western Sufi trained in Morocco told me. Sufis who talk of the unity of all religions may consider that this unity lies only in Islam, which in their view synthesized all previous religions and went beyond them, and they may still be promoting conversion to Islam.

Most Sufi mysticism is not of the non-dualistic variety like

Vedanta or Buddhism, but emphasizes nearness to God. This I gathered from an American who studied with some of the leading Sufis in North Africa and Europe, particularly the followers of Sheikh Al-Allawi. The highest stage of Sufism called fana, has sometimes been equated with Nirvana of the Buddhists or realization of Brahman of the Hindus because it means annihilation. Yet to most Sufis it means annihilation of any separate will apart from Allah. It does not mean complete mergence into Allah or the experience "I am Allah." It means becoming wholly dependent upon Allah and recognizing oneself to be a servant of God. Sufi attainment usually consists of going to the higher regions of Heaven or Paradise and being close to God. They seldom recognize the Self (Atman) as the ultimate spiritual Reality and when they do it may be owing to a Vedantic influence.

Some Sufis, particularly in India, have freely mingled with yogis but they are exceptional. Most Sufis themselves like to discriminate their approach from yogic spirituality, which they see as too otherworldly. Sufi spirituality is more practically oriented, more in the world, and done by householders. It tries to use the forces of the world for spiritual purposes rather than to renounce them for the spiritual life. Islam was originally a revolt against the rule of priests and monks, a sort of religion of ordinary people, and Sufi mysticism follows this trend. Sufis usually have families and work in the world. Great Sufis have been perfumers, poets, calligraphers, merchants, and even generals, but seldom ascetics and not monks.

One common Sufi quote is that Mohammed said that there will be no monkery in Islam. While Islam and Sufism have glorified the conquests of generals and taken soldiers into their ranks, they have criticized the practices of monks. Built into Islam and to Sufism based upon it is a spiritual approach active in the world and seeking to convert the world to its views. Hence Sufi mysticism has often turned into militancy or missionary activity. In this regard it may emphasize social activity and group work over individual spiritual practice.

However, that Sufism is not usually another form of yogic spirituality does not mean that it has no value. The Sufis possess a great and beautiful literature and much occult and spiritual knowledge, including much they have retained from the pre-Islamic period. The liberal Sufis have been perhaps the most important spiritual tradition in the greater Western world. They have been the main caretakers of the older mystical traditions of the Western world and for the West to awaken spiritually it must rediscover this tradition. Yet the orientation, methodology and goal of the Sufis, particularly orthodox Sufis, is different from yogic approaches, and from the yogic perspective it would appear that the ultimate goal of Self-realization is not understood by many Sufis.

While some Sufis appear to have tried to spiritualize Islam, linking it up with other religions and older forms of mysticism in order to move it away from its militant and fundamentalist orthodoxy, it appears more often that orthodox Islam succeeded in either silencing the Sufis or turning them into its own instruments of conversion. Sometimes yogic like spiritual attainments were attributed to Sufis as propaganda to promote conversion to Islam. Sufis were portrayed as yogis in India to make Islam appear attractive to Hindus, not because the Sufis had achieved such inner realization or were even seeking it. Often the grave of a Sufi was placed on a Hindu temple and the power of the place was attributed to the Sufi in order to convert Hindus. Such manufactured saints were really militant people, glorified afterwards in stories for propaganda purposes.

We shouldn't be surprised by this either. Militant Sufi orders were the equivalent of priests and Jesuits in Christianity. They were very devoted to their religion and went ahead to other lands, much like spies, to learn the ways of their peoples in order to find out how better to convert them. While liberal Sufi groups appear to have opposed Islamic militancy, they do not seem to have had much affect upon it. They may never have been strong enough to really challenge it. They may have had enough work merely to protect themselves and their communities, much less to protect those of other religious beliefs even if they sympathized with them.

However much those in the yogic tradition may wish to sympathize with the Sufis and see a common spirituality in their tradition, they should not ignore the different orientation and goal of most of Sufism, or the fact that the more Sufism comes to resemble yogic spirituality, the less it appears to be part of Islam. They can take what is good in Sufism without having to uncritically accept anything that calls itself Sufi. In fact the truly mystical Sufis in India have generally been more honored by Hindus than by orthodox Muslims.

Yet even recognizing the differences that exist between yogic and Sufi spirituality Hindus would be much happier if Sufism, particularly of the liberal variety, were more influential in Islam, as with the Sufis there is ground for dialogue. They wish the Sufis well in their struggles with the militant Muslims who oppose them.

The Islamic and the Yogic Model

If we study the life of Mohammed and the teachings of the Koran, it is clear that his religious approach is different than the yogic model and should not be reduced to it. While Mohammed and the Koran may not fare entirely well if examined from the standpoint of yogic spirituality, it could also be said that yogic spirituality may not fare well if examined from the standpoint of Islam and Mohammed, who would probably consider it to be timid and overly introverted.

The Islamic model of spirituality through Mohammed is not passive, non-violent, pacifistic, otherworldly, monistic, renunciate, monastic, and inclusive like yogic traditions. It is assertive, militant, political, this worldly, monotheistic, non-monastic, and generally exclusive, though it does have its devotional, mystical and contemplative side. However we may want to interpret these differences, we cannot ignore them or reduce one to the other.

Mohammed remains one of the most important figures not only in religion but in politics and world history, but we must look at him as he presents himself, and not put him in a mold that he does not reflect. Though we can respect Mohammed as a great social leader and religious reformer, even as a mystic, it is inaccurate to interpret Mohammed as a yogi or sage in the Hindu-Buddhist sense. Whether one believes that Mohammed had a different or better way to God-realization than yogic traditions (which some Sufis say), that he had a different goal altogether and God-realization is a delusion (which most orthodox Muslims believe), or that Mohammed failed to achieve the highest realization as taught in the yogic tradition, though he may have had various mystical experiences (which appears to be the case if we apply yogic principles to his life and experience as Vivekananda did), depends upon one's point of view.

Section III

Historical Issues

3.1
India and Hinduism in the Mahabharata

One not uncommonly comes across the opinion today that India was never really a nation but that its nationhood was only recently invented by the British through their definition of the region as part of their empire. Similarly we are told that Hinduism was up to recently not a religion at all but merely various local cults and that Hinduism as a single religion was an idea developed along with the idea of India as a nation—that as a religion Hinduism is basically a creation of modern political interests. These ideas are often used to discredit India as a real country or Hinduism as a valid religion. They are used by Marxist and leftist elements or by non-Hindus to draw Hindus into their fold. However, such ideas are clearly refuted by the most important work of literature that we have from India, the Mahabharata.

The Mahabharata of 100,000 verses dates from at least two thousand years ago, though portions of it are much older, and its story goes back perhaps more than thirty-five hundred years. A version of it was noted in the Tamil Nadu region of South India as early as the first century BC. Mahabharata literally means "Great India" as Bharata is the traditional name for India.

The Mahabharata presents peoples from the entire subcontinent of India. The story centers on the conflict between the Kauravas and Pandavas, who were members of the same ruling family of the Kuru-Panchala kingdom which extended through the Ganges-Yamuna region. The mother of the Kauravas was Gandhari of Gandhara, which is now Pakistan and northeast Afghanistan. The mother of the Pandavas was Kunti of the Yadava line of what would now be Madhya Pradesh. The Pandavas were allied with Krishna who was originally a king of Mathura on the Yamuna south of Delhi, but moved his capital to Dwaraka in the southern part of his kingdom in Gujarat. Krishna's main enemy was Jarasandha, King of Magadha (Bihar). Kings of all India participated in the Mahabharata war including from Pragjyotish (Assam) and Sind. In their pilgrimages (*tīrthayātrās*) and victory marches (*digvijayas*) the Pandavas traveled all over India from Afghanistan in the west, to Tibet in the north, Assam in the east, to Kanya Kumari in the south. Sri Lanka is also mentioned.

Whether the Mahabharata is an historical account or a mere story makes no difference in this issue. The existence of such a story factually or on a literary level proves the same thing—that the idea of the subcontinent of India as a cultural unit clearly existed at a time contemporaneous with the Roman empire—long before any of the modern nation-states had come into being and long before most of Europe was even populated. The Mahabharata reflects that India as a cultural unit already formed some two thousand years ago. In this regard no nation, subcontinent or religion has an epic of such proportion or which reflects the integration of such a large region as India through the Mahabharata. There is no such epic as Great Europe or Great China. There is no great epic of Christianity or Islam that encompasses such a clearly defined cultural region which still exists today. Based on the evidence of the Mahabharata it could be argued that India is perhaps the oldest nation in the world.

It is the same case with Hinduism as a religion. Hinduism as we know it today is basically the same religion taught in the Mahabharata. The Mahabharata presents a synthesis of the worship of the great Hindu Gods of Shiva, Vishnu and the Goddess

(Devi), as well as the lesser figures of Ganesh, Skanda, and Surya. Their worship is integrated on an earlier Brahmanical basis and a respect for the Vedas, the Vedic Rishis and the Upanishads, which includes the great truths of Vedanta. The Mahabharata makes Krishna into a great teacher and avatar as well as recognizes Rama and the other avatars of Vishnu. The Mahabharata presents a synthesis of the teachings of Vedanta, Sankhya and Yoga. It contains teachings on the duties of kings, classes and stages of life, medicine and astrology. In fact it compasses all the domains of knowledge and all the issues of human life and culture. It is not just a religious book but the document for an entire civilization.

Interestingly the Mahabharata does not present itself as a new religion or cultural document but as a development of the older Vedic tradition. Even in the older Upanishads and the Brahmanas kings and sages are mentioned from such diverse regions as Gandhara (Afghanistan), Videha (eastern Bihar and Nepal) and Vidarbha (Maharashtra). This is a considerably larger region than the Bible which reflects mainly the people of the small country of Palestine or the Koran which reflects the Arabs of Mecca and Medina. The Vedas also present a much great diversity of personages, with many great sages and yogis, rather than a few prophets only.

We must note that when the Mahabharata was televised in India a few years ago, the entire country was mesmerized. Trains stopped. Government offices were closed to allow people to watch the program. A comparable phenomenon has never occurred in the West when films of the Bible were shown on television, nor has any other national epic so gripped the attention of any country. This shows that the Mahabharata still unites the country and is indeed a national epic.

Those who would deny any real history to India as a nation or Hinduism as a religion have only to look at the Mahabharata to see the absurdity of their views. Even the title of the book challenges their view.

3.2

The Aryan Invasion of India Questioned in the Western Textbooks

According to the Aryan Invasion Theory—which is the basis of interpreting the ancient history of India found in most books today—the Vedic people were barbarian hordes who overran North India after 1500 BC. They destroyed the more advanced Dravidian civilization of the subcontinent, which is evidenced by the ruins of the Harappan or Indus civilization. This theory is diametrically opposed to the traditional Hindu view of Vedic culture which regards it as indigenous from India, arising on the Sarasvati river west of Delhi, and sees it as a culture of great spirituality ruled by seers and yogis.

The invasion idea was invented by nineteenth century European thinkers, and was mixed with colonial and missionary policies. It was always questioned by Hindus, including great thinkers like Sri Aurobindo, Vivekananda, B.G. Tilak and Dayananda Sarasvati. It had no basis in the extensive Vedic and Puranic literature which speaks of no outside origin for the Vedic people. Yet owing to the European intellectual domination of the world, which followed its political domination, this idea became regarded as the truth. It reduced the ancient history of India to a brutal invasion and coverup, with the perpetrators given the mantle of sages by the ignorance of later generations!

Recently, however, this idea has been challenged again by a

number of scholars east and west. Its opponents are becoming increasingly more numerous, raising more and more objections, showing new astronomical, archeological, skeletal and geological evidence in favor of dismissing the theory. Meanwhile there has been no substantial evidence to support the theory apart from the uncertainty of linguistic speculation. Everything that has been proposed to support it has been found not to have really occurred or to have other causes.

For examples, the Harappan cities were found to have been abandoned by climate and river changes, not destroyed by outside invaders, and the horse, thought to have been first brought by the invading Aryans has been now been found to have existed already in many Harappan sites. Contrary to the theory, the picture has emerged of an indigenous and organic development of civilization in ancient India going back to 6500 BC (the Mehrgarh site in Pakistan) with no break in continuity and no significant outside invasions or migrations. Indeed it appears that in the coming years the Aryan invasion theory will soon be discarded all over the world.

Recently the monthly newspaper *Hinduism Today* (Dec. 1994) has come out against the Aryan Invasion Theory in its Time Line edition. *Hinduism Today* is largest circulating Hindu monthly in the world. *Hinduism Today* is published in the United States, though distributed world wide, including in India.

In defense of the theory, however, people point to the fact that it is still found in textbooks throughout the world, including in India, so that such new data against it does not appear to have been accepted. Opponents of the theory have claimed that much of the data disproving it is new and has not yet had time to reach textbooks, which usually represent information some decades old. Yet now the demise of the Aryan invasion theory is entering into the textbooks.

It is strange to see, however, that the first major university textbook to seriously question the theory has not come from

India but from the West. In his recent edition of *Survey of Hinduism* (Suny, State University of New York Press 1994), Professor Klaus Klostermaier has noted important objections to this theory. He suggests that the weight of evidence is against it and that it should no longer be regarded as the main model of interpreting ancient India. *Survey of Hinduism* is perhaps the main textbook used in North America for university courses on the study of Hinduism.

Klostermaier is not a Hindu, in fact he is a Catholic priest. He is not speaking relative to any Hindu agenda but as a scholar and academician. Though as a teacher of Hinduism he appears to have some sympathy with the tradition, he cannot be regarded as promoting Hinduism. He is critical of Hindu beliefs and practices in different parts of his book. But the Aryan Invasion Theory is something he questions on the evidence.

He states (pg. 34): "Both the spatial and the temporal extent of the Indus civilization has expanded dramatically on the basis of new excavations and the dating of the Vedic age as well as the theory of an Aryan invasion of India has been shaken. We are required to completely reconsider not only certain aspects of Vedic India, but the entire relationship between Indus civilization and Vedic culture." Later he adds (pg. 38): "The certainty seems to be growing that the Indus civilization was carried by the Vedic Indians, who were not invaders from Southern Russia but indigenous for an unknown period of time in the lower Central Himalayan regions."

He questions the difference proposed between Vedic and Indus culture and shows a continuity or possibility of identity between the two. He mentions the data on the Sarasvati river, which according to scientific studies dried up around 1900 BC. As the Sarasvati is the main river of the Vedas, he states (pg. 36): "If, As Muller suggested, the Aryan invasion took place around 1500 BC, it does not make much sense to locate villages along the banks of the by then dried up Sarasvati."

He notes skeletal information that shows a continuity of the same racial and ethnic groups in ancient India as today, thus refuting the idea that India was populated by an outside race in the ancient period. He notes the discovery of the ancient city of Dwaraka in Gujarat, the reputed city of Krishna, and its date to 1500 BC. He notes astronomical evidence in Vedic texts that suggest early calendars contemporaneous with the Indus era.

He has been most influenced by the work of Subhash Kak and quotes him in several places, including Kak's decoding of what he calls "the astronomical code of the Vedas." He also mentions from my work on the subject, as presented in my book *Gods, Sages and Kings: Vedic Secrets of Ancient Civilization.* He quotes one long passage of Kak (pg. 38): by the middle of the fourth millennium BCE the Indo-European and the Dravidian worlds had already interacted and met across Northwest India and the plateau of Iran....The Indo-European world at this time must already have stretched from Europe to North India and just below it lay the Dravidian people. The interaction for centuries between these two powerful peoples gave rise to the Vedic language, which, though structurally Indo-European, was greatly influenced by the Dravidian language. The Vedic civilization was a product of the civilization of these two peoples as was the Harappan civilization.

These arguments represent the new data coming from various archaeologists and Vedic scholars. They do not come from Klostermaier, but clearly they are strong enough to produce a case that even Western academicians now have to listen to. They have caused Klostermaier to question the whole Western reading of the Vedas. "We can be certain that these first efforts to get away from a historicist-humanistic Western reading of the Vedas will be followed by more detailed analyses and probably quite startling discovers about the character and content of Vedic civilization. (pg.38)"

The same arguments have been raised in India by many

writers, archaeologists, scientists and spiritual leaders, but still have not yet entered into the textbooks. Now the question arises, *if textbooks in the West can be changed in regard to the Aryan Invasion Theory, why cannot textbooks in India be changed*, particularly as the theory has frequently been used to discredit the culture of India and the Hindu religion? We would expect that textbooks in India would be the first to change on this matter and not have to follow those in the West. Surely if new data arose in a Western country like Greece, showing the greater antiquity of its ancient civilization and literature, the entire country would be quick to proclaim the new information.

Unfortunately India does not appear to want to acknowledge its past, particularly if it gives credence to its spiritual tradition which a number of groups oppose. The Aryan Invasion Theory has become a matter of political importance in the country, and politics is always willing to twist things for its electoral needs.

The British rulers of colonial India, Marxists scholars and politicians, Dravidian nationalists, Caste Reform advocates of various types, Christian missionaries and Muslim groups have used the invasion theory to discredit or divide Hindu culture, particularly to attack its Brahmanical side. Even today one can see "Brahmins go home (to Central Asia)," painted on walls as political propaganda in south India. Dravidians, the lower castes, and Muslims have all at times identified themselves with the pre-Aryan indigenous people of India whom the invading Aryans were supposed to have conquered and enslaved. Clearly several groups have part of their identity invested in the invasion theory that would be disconcerting to lose. On the other hand, many of the founders of the Indian independence movement like Tilak and Aurobindo wrote against the theory. It appeared important to them in restoring Indian identity to reestablish the credibility of ancient Indian civilization and its continuity.

Yet whatever one's social views, history should not be subject to them but should be examined according to the facts. Now the facts severely question the Aryan Invasion Theory, so that it should no longer be portrayed as the truth. The events in a country today should not be made hostage to its history of over four thousand years ago, whatever it might have been. Only in India does this occur. Yet India must now look at its ancient history anew, in the light of the collapse of the invasion theory. A greater continuity to Indian civilization is revealed that hopefully can bring more wholeness to the country.

If the Aryan Invasion Theory is not true it means that India is the oldest most continuous civilization in the world, with the oldest and most extensive literature (the Vedas), and is therefore one of the great centers of world civilization rivalling those of Egypt and Babylonia. It is a heritage to be proud of, however one may wish to interpret it.

3.3
The Aryan-Dravidian Divide

The British ruled India, as they did other lands, by a divide and conquer strategy. They promoted religious, ethnic and cultural divisions among their colonies to keep them under control. Unfortunately these policies entered into the intellectual and religious realms. The same simplistic ideas that were used for political domination were applied for interpreting the culture and history of India, as dividing a culture intellectually is the key to controlling it in the political realm. Regrettably many Hindus have come to believe these foreign ideas, even though a deeper examination reveals they have no real objective or scientific basis.

One of the most important of these European-invented ideas is that India is a land of two races—the lighter-skinned Aryans and the darker-skinned Dravidians—and that the Dravidians were the original inhabitants of India whom the invading Aryans conquered and dominated. From this came the idea that what is called Hindu culture was originally Dravidian, and only latter was borrowed by the Aryans who, however, never gave the Dravidians proper credit for it. This idea has been used to turn the people of South India against the people of North India—as if the southerners were a different and maligned race—and has been used to create resentment between them.

Modern Dravidian politicians have unfortunately taken up

this European idea and used it for the purposes of Dravidian nationalism, placing the Dravidians against the North Indians or Aryans, and trying to recreate the purity of Dravidian culture by eliminating so-called Aryan influences, like the Vedas, which are regarded as foreign. In this process they don't realize that they are only promoting a modern European idea of who they are, not any original heritage. They are basing their Dravidian nationalism not on their own culture or history but on a recent invention of colonial thought.

Racial Theories

The nineteenth century was the era of European imperialism. Many Europeans believed that they belonged to a superior race and that their religion, Christianity, was a superior religion compared to which all other religions were barbaric, particularly a religion like Hinduism which used many idols. The Europeans felt that it was their duty to convert non-Christians, sometimes even it required intimidation, force or bribery (we might add that this mentality and its effects are still in operation in a number of missionary efforts in India today). They saw non-Christians like children who had to be disciplined in order to become really civilized (that is, to become like the Europeans).

European thinkers of the era were dominated by a racial theory of man, which was interpreted primarily in terms of color. They saw themselves as belonging to a superior "white" or Caucasian race. They had enslaved the Negroid or "black" race. As Hindus were also dark or "colored," they were similarly deemed inferior. The British thus, not surprisingly, looked upon the culture of India in a similar way as having been a land of a lighter-skinned or Aryan race (the North Indians), ruling a dark or Dravidian race (the South Indians).

About this time in history similarities between Indo-European languages became evident. Sanskrit and the languages of North India were found to be relatives of the languages of Europe, while the Dravidian languages of South India appeared to be of another language family. By the racial theory, Europeans naturally felt that the speakers of any original Indo-European language must have been "white," as they were not prepared to recognize that their languages could have been derived from darker-skinned Hindus. As all Hindus were dark compared to the Europeans, it was assumed that the original white Indo-European invaders of India must have been assimilated by the dark indigenous population, and they left their mark more on north India where people have a lighter complexion.

The Nazis later took this idea of a white Aryan superior race to its extreme of brutality, but they did not invent the idea, nor were they the only ones to use it for purposes of exploitation. They took what was a common idea of nineteenth century European thought. They perverted this idea further, but the distortion of it was already the basis of much exploitation and misunderstanding.

The Racial Interpretation of the Vedas

European Vedic interpreters used the racial idea to explain the Vedas. The Vedas speak of a battle between light and darkness, between the Sun God and his manifestations and the demons of darkness. This was turned into a war between light-skinned Aryans and dark-skinned Dravidians. Such scholars did not bother to examine the fact that most religions and mythologies—including those of the Ancient American Indians, Egyptians, Greeks and Persians—have such an idea of a battle between the forces of light and darkness (which is the symbolic conflict between truth and falsehood), but we do not interpret their statements racially. In short, Europeans projected racism into the history of India, and accused the Hindus of the very racism that they themselves were using to dominate the Hindus.

European scholars pointed out that caste in India was originally defined by color, which is how they translated the Sanskrit term *varṇa*, the basis of caste. In Vedic thought Brahmins are said to be white, Kshatriyas (warriors) red, Vaishyas (merchants) yellow, and Shudras (servants) black. Hence the Brahmins were deemed to have been originally the white Aryans and the Dravidians the dark Shudras, whom the Aryans enslaved. However, the colors of the different classes refers only to the *guṇas* or qualities of each class, which represent different energetic types of human being. White is the color of purity (*sattva guṇa*), dark that of impurity (*tamoguṇa*), red the color of action (*rajoguṇa*), and yellow the color of trade (also *rajoguṇa*). To turn this into races is simplistic and incorrect. Where is the red race and where is the yellow race in India? And when have the Kshatriyas been a red race and the Vaishyas a yellow race?

The racial idea reached yet more ridiculous proportions. Vedic passages speaking of their enemies (mainly demons) as without nose (*anāsa*), were interpreted as a racial slur against the snub-nosed Dravidians. Now Dravidians are not snub-nosed or low-nosed people, and many Dravidians have as prominent noses as anyone in the North of India. The same Vedic demons are also described as footless (*apāda*). Where is such a footless and noseless race and what does it have to do with the Dravidians? Moreover Vedic Gods like Agni (fire), who are called Aryans, are described as footless and headless (*apāda, ashīrsha*). Where are such headless and footless Aryans? Yet such "scholarship" can be found in prominent Western books on the history of India, some published in India and used in schools in India to the present day.

This idea was taken further and Hindu Gods like Krishna, whose name means dark, or Shiva who is portrayed as dark in complexion, were said to have originally been Dravidian Gods taken over by the invading Aryans (under the simplistic idea that Dravidians as dark-skinned people must have worshipped dark colored Gods). Yet Kriśhna and Shiva are not black but dark blue. Where is such a dark blue race? Moreover the different

Hindu Gods, like the different classes, have different colors relative to their qualities. Lakshmi is portrayed as pink, Saraswati as white, Kali as blue-black, or Yama, the God of death, as green. Where have such races been in India or elsewhere?

In a similar light, some scholars pointed out that Vedic Gods like Savitar have golden hair and golden skin, showing blond and fair-skinned people living in ancient India. However, Savitar is a Sun God and Sun Gods are usually gold in color, as has been the case of the ancient Egyptian, Mayan and Inca and other Sun Gods. Who has a black or blue Sun God? This is from the simple fact that the Sun has a golden color. What does this have to do with race? And why should it be a racial statement in the Vedas but not elsewhere?

The Term Aryan

A number of European scholars of the nineteenth century, such as Max Muller, did state that Aryan is not a racial term and there is no evidence that it ever was so used in the Vedas, but their views on this matter were ignored. We should clearly note that there is no place in Hindu literature wherein Aryan has ever been equated with a race or with a particular set of physical characteristics. The term Arya means "noble" or "spiritual," and has been so used by Buddhist, Jains and Zoroastrians as well as Hindus. Religions that have called themselves Aryan have had members of many different races. Race was never a bar for anyone joining some form of the Arya Dharma or teaching of noble people.

Aryan is a term similar in meaning to the Sanskrit word Sri, an epithet of respect. We could equate it with the English word Sir. We cannot imagine that a race of men named sir took over England in the Middle Ages and dominated the common people who were a different race, because most of the people in power in the country were called sir. Yet this is the kind of thinking that has been superimposed upon the history of India.

New Evidence on the Indus Culture

The Indus civilization—the ancient urban culture of north India in the third millennium BC—has been interpreted as a Dravidian or non-Aryan culture. Though this has never been proved, it has been taken by many people to be a fact. However, new archeological evidence shows that the so-called Indus culture was a Vedic culture, centered not on the Indus but on the banks of the Sarasvati river of Vedic fame (the culture should be renamed not the Indus but the "Sarasvati culture"), and that its language was also related to Sanskrit. The ancient Sarasvati dried up around 1900 BC. Hence the Vedic texts that speak so eloquently of this river must predate this period.

The racial types found in the Indus civilization are now found to have been generally the same as those of north India today, and that there is no evidence of any significant intrusive populations into India in the Indus or post-Indus era. This new information tends to either dismiss the Aryan invasion theory or to place it back at such an early point in history (before 3000 BC or even 6000 BC), that it has little bearing on what we know as the culture of India.

Aryan and Dravidian Races

The idea of Aryan and Dravidian races is the product of an unscientific culturally biased form of thinking that saw race in terms of color. There are, scientifically speaking, no such things as Aryan or Dravidian races. The three primary races are the Caucasian, the Mongolian and the Negroid. Both the Aryans and Dravidians are related branches of the Caucasian race, generally placed in the same Mediterranean subbranch. The difference between the so-called Aryans of the north and Dravidians of the south is a difference in skin color, but this is not a racial division. Biologically both the North and South Indians are of the same Caucasian race, only when closer to the equator the skin becomes darker, and under the influence of constant heat the bodily frame tends to become a little smaller. While we can speak of some ethnic differences between North and South Indian peoples, they are only secondary.

For example, if we take a typical person from Punjab, another from Maharashtra, and a third from Tamil Nadu we will find that the Maharashtrians generally fall in between the other two in terms of build and skin color. We see a gradual shift of characteristics from north to south, but no real different race. An Aryan and Dravidian race in India is no more real than a north and a south European race. Those who use such terms are misusing language. We would just as well place the blond Swede of Europe in a different race from the darker haired and browner skinned person of southern Italy.

Nor is the Caucasian race the "white" race. Caucasians can be of any color from pure white to almost pure black, with every shade of brown in between. The predominant Caucasian type found in the world is not the blond-blue-eyed northern European but the black hair, brown-eyed darker skinned Mediterranean type such as we find from southern Europe to north India. Similarly the Mongolian race is not yellow. Many Chinese have skin whiter than many so-called Caucasians. In fact of all the races, the Caucasian is the most variable in its skin color. Yet many of the identification forms that people fill out in the world today still define race in terms of color.

North and South Indian Religions

Scholars dominated by the Aryan-Dravidian racial idea have tried to make some Hindu Gods Dravidian (Non-Aryan) and other Hindu Gods Aryan (Vedic), even though there is no such division within Hinduism. This is based upon a superficial identification of deities with color, Krishna as black and therefore Dravidian, which we have already shown the incorrectness of (to think that sages or deities were named only after the color of their racial stock). In the Mahabharata, Krishna traces his lineage through the Vedic line of the Yadus, a famous Aryan people of the south and west of India, and there are instances as far back as the Rig Veda of seers whose name meant dark (like Krishna Angirasa or Shyava Atreya).

Early investigators thought they saw a Shaivite element in the so-called Dravidian Indus Valley civilization, with the existence of Shiva linga like sacred objects, and seals resembling Shiva. However further examination has also found large numbers of Vedic like fire-altars replete with all the traditional offers as found in the Hindu literature known as the *Brāhmaṇas*, again refuting such simplistic divisions. The religion of the Indus (Sarasvati) culture appears to include many Vedic as well as Puranic elements (note also the article on the Unity of the Vedic and Shaivite Religions).

Aryan and Dravidian Languages

The Indo-European languages and the Dravidian do have important differences. Their ways of developing words and grammar are different. However, it is a misnomer to call all Indo-European languages Aryan. The Sanskrit term Aryan would not apply to European languages, which are materialistic in orientation, because Aryan in Sanskrit means spiritual. When the term Aryan is used as indicating certain languages, the term is being used in a Western or European sense that we should remember is quite apart from its traditional Sanskrit meaning, and implies a racial bias that the Sanskrit term does not have.

We can speak of Indo-European and Dravidian languages, but this does not necessarily mean that Aryan and Dravidian must differ in culture, race or religion. The Hungarians and Finns of Europe are of a different language group than the other Europeans, but we do not speak of them as of a Finnish race, or the Finns as being non-Europeans, nor do we consider that their religious beliefs must therefore be unrelated to those of the rest of Europe.

Even though Dravidian languages are based on a different model than Sanskrit, there are thirty to seventy percent Sanskrit words in south Indian languages like Telugu and Tamil, which is a much higher percentage than north Indian languages like Hindi. In addition both North and South Indian languages have a similar construction and phraseology which links them close together, that European languages do not share. This has caused some linguists even to propose that Hindi was a Dravidian language. In short, the language compartments, like the racial ones, are not as rigid as has been thought.

In fact if we examine the oldest Vedic Sanskrit, we find similar sounds to Dravidian languages (the cerebral letters, for example), which are not present in other Indo-European tongues. This shows either that there already were Dravidians in the same region as the Vedic people, and part of the same culture with them, or that Dravidian languages could also have been early offshoots of Sanskrit, which was the theory of the modern rishi, Sri Aurobindo. In addition the traditional inventor of the Dravidian languages was said to have been Agastya, one of the most important rishis of the Rig Veda, the oldest Sanskrit text. The oldest forms of Dravidian languages are written in Brahmi, the script for Sanskrit, and contain much influence of Sanskrit as well.

The Dravidians in Vedic and Puranic Lore

Some Vedic texts, like the Aitareya Brahmana or Manu Samhita, have looked at the Dravidians as people who have fallen from Vedic values and practices. However, they do not look at them as indigenous or different people but as descendants of Vedic kings, notably Vishvamitra, who have taken upon unorthodox practices. These same texts look unfavorably upon certain peoples of North India, like the Mahabharata criticizing peoples of Sind and Sauvira or west India as unaryan, as deviating from Vedic culture, even though such people were obviously

Indo-European in language.

Other texts like the Ramayana portray the Dravidians, the inhabitants of Kishkindha (modern Karnataka), as allies of Aryan kings like Rama. Hence there appears to have been periods in history when the Dravidians or some portion of them were not looked on with favor by some followers of Vedic culture, but this was only temporary. If we look through the history of India, there has been a time when almost every part of India has been dominated by unorthodox traditions like the Buddhist, Jain or Persian (Zoroastrian), not to mention outside religions like Islam or Christianity, or dominated by other foreign conquerors, like the Greeks, Scythians (Shakas) or Huns. That Gujarat was a once suspect land to Vedic people when it was under Jain domination does not cause us to turn the Gujaratis into another race or religion. That something similar happened to the Dravidians at a point in history does not require making them permanently non-Aryan. In the history of Europe, for example, that Austria once went through a Protestant phase, does not cause modern Austrians to consider that they cannot be Catholics.

The kings of South India, like the Chola and Pandya dynasties, relate their lineages back to Manu. The Matsya Purana moreover makes Manu, the progenitor of all the Aryas, originally a South Indian king, Satyavrata. Therefore there are not only traditions that make the Dravidians descendants of Vedic rishis and kings, but those that make the Aryans of North India descendants of Dravidian kings. The two cultures are so intimately related that it is difficult to say which came first. Any differences between them appear to be secondary, and nothing exists like the great racial divide that the Aryan-Dravidian idea has promoted.

The Dravidians as Preservers of Vedic Culture

Through the long and cruel Islamic assault on India, South India became the land of refuge for Vedic culture, and to a great extent remains so to the present day. The best Vedic chanting, rituals and other traditions are preserved in South India. It is ironic therefore that the best preservers of Aryan culture in India have been branded as non-Aryan.

Dravidians do not have to feel that Vedic culture is any more foreign to them than it is to the people of North India. They need not feel that they are racially different than the people of the north. They need not feel that they are losing their original culture by using Sanskrit. Nor need they feel that they have to assert themselves against north India or Vedic culture to protect their real heritage.

Hindu culture has never suppressed indigenous cultures or been opposed to cultural variations, as have the monolithic conversion religions of Christianity and Islam. The Vedic rishis and yogis encouraged the development of local traditions. They established sacred places in all the regions in which their culture spread. They did not make everyone have to visit a single holy place like Mecca, Rome or Jerusalem. Nor did they find local or tribal deities as something to be eliminated as heathen or pagan. They respected the common human aspiration for the Divine that we find in all cultures and encouraged diversity and uniqueness in our approach to it.

The people of North India also need not take this north/south division as something fundamental. It is not a racial difference that makes the skin of south Indians darker but merely the effect of climate. Any racial group living in the tropics for some centuries or millennia would eventually turn dark. And whatever color a person's skin may be has nothing to do with their true nature according to the Vedas that see the same Self or Atman in all.

Nor is it necessary to turn various Vedic Gods into Dravidian Gods to give the Dravidians equality with the so-called Aryans in terms of the numbers or antiquity of their Gods. This only gives credence to what is a superficial distinction in the first place. What is necessary is to assert what is truly Aryan in the culture of India, North or South, which is high on spiritual values in character and action. These occur not only in the Vedas but also the Agamas and other scriptures of the greater tradition.

The Aryans and Dravidians are part of the same culture and we need not speak of them as separate. Dividing them and placing them at odds with each other serves the interests of neither but only damages their common culture (which is what those who propound these ideas are often seeking). It is time, therefore, to look beyond the Aryan-Dravidian difference, which is much smaller than believed, and look to the greater commonality of Hindu culture.

3.4
The Unity of the Vedic and Shaivite Religions

There has been an effort to divide the Hindu religion into two hostile camps by opposing Shaivism, the worship of Lord Shiva, versus Brahmanism or the Vedic tradition, as two separate and conflicting religions in India. This has arisen as part of a general tendency to interpret the diversity of Hinduism not as a universalist approach—which is the Hindu view—but as a collection of contrary cults artificially put together.

Shaivism has been regarded by many, particularly Western scholars, as Dravidian; that is, as an ethnic religion of South Indians, while the Vedic tradition has been labelled as Aryan or the ethnic religion of North Indians (meaning Aryan race, though Aryan is nowhere a racial term in Sanskrit). According to the Aryan invasion theory the North Indians were invaders and the South Indians or Dravidians were the original people of the subcontinent. Shaivism thereby has been regarded as the indigenous religion, while Brahmanism has been turned into a product of the invading Aryans. This reduction of religions to ethnic cults is highly questionable in itself and appears more as a political manipulation than any spiritual inquiry. Such scholars, moreover, have failed to really examine the Vedic and Shaivite teachings. What they propose as major differences between the two are only variations of name and form.

Dravidian Shaivism has been called the religion of South India as opposed to the Vedic Aryan religion of North India. While there are cultural variations between North and South India, this division is simplistic and misleading. The idea of "Dravidian Shaivism" implies two points; first that Dravidians are primarily Shaivites, and second that Shaivites are primarily Dravidians. The truth is that neither position is valid. Shaivism is an important tradition in South India, but to oppose it to other traditions in India is totally unnecessary and very misleading.

Dravidians have as commonly been Vaishnavas or worshippers of Lord Vishnu, as they have been Shaivites, or worshippers of Lord Shiva. There are long lineages of Dravidian Vaishnava saints and kings going back into ancient history. Other religious teachings from India, both orthodox and non-orthodox, have also been popular in South India through history. Both Buddhism and Jainism, which also styled themselves Aryan religions, had large followings in South India during the historical period. Kanchipuram, the main sacred city of South India, was divided into four quarters: a Vaishnava quarter, a Shaiva quarter, a Buddhist quarter, and a Jain quarter. In addition many Brahmanical traditions have flourished in South India and South India remains today the chief site of Brahmanical learning and Vedic chanting. There is nothing to suggest that Dravidians have been exclusively Shaivites or that Shaivism in South India was opposed to other Hindu teachings, or is fundamentally different from them. On the contrary, South Indian Shaivism appears as an integral part of the greater Shaivite and Hindu traditions of all India and beyond.

Relative to the second point, the worship of Shiva has been popular throughout India and wherever Indian culture and spiritual traditions have traveled, like Indonesia and Indochina. In fact, the most famous sites of Shiva worship are, as is commonly known, in North India. These include Kashmir in the far northwest, Kailas in what is now Tibet, Gangotri and Kedarnath in the central Himalayan region, and Kashi or Varanasi (Benares) on the Ganges. When have these ever been known as primarily Dravidian holy sites? Shiva is portrayed as a Himalayan Deity with the Ganges river descending on his head. Therefore the idea that Shaivism is uniquely Dravidian also has little foundation.

Shaivism in South India may differ a little from that of North India, but in all Hindu teachings there are always many local variations as part of the richness of the tradition. Vaishnavism is a little different in Gujarat than in Bengal. Shaivism in Kashmir is a little different than Shaivism in Varanasi. Devi worship in South India is a little different from that of Bengal or Kashmir. Must these all be turned into different races or religions?

Archeological evidence over the last ten years has disproved the idea of an invasion of Indo-European peoples (Aryans) into India in ancient times. The civilization of ancient India, of the Indus Valley, has now been proved to have been centered on the Sarasvati river of Vedic fame, which went dry around 1900 BC. Hence the Vedas must be earlier than the drying up of this river and must be indigenous to India as the image of the Sarasvati pervades all of the Vedas back to the oldest parts of the Rig Veda. In addition, from the Mehrgarh site of 6500 BC to the civilization of the Ganges area after 900 BC can be traced a continuity of people and customs, and no evidence of any major intrusive new populations. Such finds confirm Vedic astronomical symbolism that mentions equinoctial and solstice positions going back to 2500 BC (the Krittika, Pleiades or Taurus vernal equinox) and earlier. In light of this new evidence we should examine the proposed differences between the Vedic and Shaivite religions, which have been based upon the invasion theory, particularly the difference between Shiva and Indra, the main Vedic God.

Those who divide Shaivism from the Vedas like to compare the deity Shiva in the Puranas with the diminished role of Indra, the greatest of the Vedic Gods, in these texts. As Shiva is the great deity of the Puranas and Indra is no more than the Lord of Heaven, some scholars have concluded that the Vedic religion was demoted and reduced in favor of an indigenous Shaivite tradition. This idea has been a source of much error. However if we compare the role of Indra in the Vedas with that of Shiva in the Puranas, a much different story emerges. While Shiva and Indra in the Puranas are very different, we find a remarkable similarity between Vedic Indra and Puranic Shiva. Vedic Indra and Puranic Shiva share many of the same names and functions, so much so that the two figures cannot be divided from one another. Much of the following information comes from Ganapati Muni, the chief disciple of the great South Indian guru Ramana Maharshi, who wrote a small treatise in Sanskrit on the identity of Indra and Shiva (*Indreshvarābheda Sūtra*).

Indra means the Lord or ruler, so does Ishvara, an important name for Shiva. In many Vedic hymns the term Indra is used as general term for Lord, just as Ishvara is used in many Puranic hymns. Both Indra and Shiva are lauded as the supreme deity and the ruler of all the other Gods. Shiva is the great God, Mahadeva. Indra is the king of the Gods, Devaraja.

Shiva is the destroyer among the trinity of Puranic deities, which includes Brahma, the Creator, and Vishnu, the Preserver. Indra in the Vedas is a destructive God, a destroyer of obstructions (Vritra, the enemy of Indra, literally means obstruction). Indra is the destroyer of cities, Purandara: Shiva is the destroyer of the three cities, Tripurahara. We should note that because of Indra's role as destroyer of cities, there has been an attempt to make him into a deity of invading nomadic people, smashing the cities of the indigenous Dravidians (current evidence, however, does not show the destruction of any city in the Harappan civilization by outside invaders). In any case by the same logic Shiva must also be a deity of invading nomadic people, not of indigenous city dwellers. In fact in Puranic literature Shiva destroys the cities for the benefit of Indra.

Indra and Shiva both have a consort named power (Shakti in the case of Shiva, Shachi in the case of Indra), who herself is a fierce Goddess. Indra's consort Indrani is in fact the Goddess of the army in the Vedic tradition. The martial role of Shiva's consort as Durga or Chandi, the destroyer of all enemies and opposition, and the leader of the Divine army is well known. Indra and Shiva are both renowned as destroyers of demons and have terrible or wrathful forms. Indra in the Vedas is frequently called Ugra, Ghora, and Bhima which are common names for Shiva in later times, which mean fierce or terrible.

Shiva is said to be a non-Vedic God because he fights with Vedic Gods like Bhaga and Pushan and destroys the sacrifice of Daksha, who is the son of Brahma or Prajapati, from which he is excluded. Yet this Puranic myth is not entirely new. A similar story occurs in the Brahmanas as Rudra slaying Prajapati or Brahma with his arrow, which story is echoed in some hymns of the Rig Veda as well.

Indra similarly kills the son of Tvashtar, who symbolizes the sacrifice. Tvashtar is identified with Prajapati or Brahma in Vedic and Puranic thought. After slaying of the son of Tvashtar, Tvashtar tries to exclude Indra from the drinking of the Soma, much like Shiva's being excluded from getting any share of the sacrifice. Indra elsewhere destroys his own father (who is Tvashtar) and fights against the Gods. Ultimately all the Gods abandon Indra and he has to slay the dragon (Vritra) alone. By Brahmanical and Puranic accounts Vritra is a Brahmin and Indra commits the great sin of slaying a Brahmin by slaying Vritra, for which he must seek atonement.

Indra like Shiva is a fierce God who transcends good and evil, including all social customs, and does what is forbidden. Indra does things like eating meat and drinking Soma (in enormous quantities), and goes into various states of intoxication and ecstasy. Indra is born as an outcast and in some hymns in the Vedas grants favor to outcasts. Shiva similarly is a deity of ecstasy

(Soma) and transcends all social customs, often going against caste and custom.

Yet if we pursue the same logic with Indra as Western scholars have with Shiva, as fighting with the Gods, slaying Tvashtar (the deity of the sacrifice) or his son, being excluded from drinking the Soma, slaying a Brahmin, being an outcast and doing what is forbidden, Indra must also be a non-Vedic or non-Aryan God. While there has been a tendency to make Shiva into non-Vedic for having such fierce, unusual traits and unorthodox actions, Indra has the same traits. However we cannot make Indra non-Vedic because he has the largest number of hymns in the Vedas. Hence there is no reason why Shiva should be non-Vedic for having such traits either. These bizarre metaphors merely express the nature of the higher Self or Atman which transcends all the dualities and limitations of the manifest world, even that of good and evil.

Shiva has been criticized by some Hindus as unaryan. Western scholars, caught in a superficial racial view of the term Aryan, have taken this to mean that Shiva is the deity of a different race or religion. If we look to the original meaning of Aryan, which is pure or noble, calling Shiva unaryan merely refers to his fierce or terrible traits like his matted hair, his garland of snakes, and his retinue of ghosts. Shiva is not the form of God who represents ideal or noble traits, which is usually the role of Vishnu, but the form of God who represents transcendence of all dualities. Yet Indra is also to be viewed in this same light.

Indra and Shiva share yet many other traits. Indra and Shiva are both called the dancer and are associated with music and song. The letters of the Sanskrit alphabet come forth from Shiva's drum. Indra in the Vedas is called the bull of the chants, and all songs go to him like rivers to the sea. Shiva is identified in Tantric thought with the vowels of the alphabet. Indra in the Chandogya Upanishad is identified with the vowels among the letters of the alphabet. Shiva is identified with the mantra OM. Indra in the Vedas and Upanishads is also identified with the OM.

Shiva is a mountain God, so is Indra a God of the mountains. Shiva allows the heavenly Ganges river to descend on his head. Indra's main action is destroying the clouds (mountains, glaciers) to allow the rivers to flow from the mountains into the sea. Both deities are interwoven with the myth of the descent of the heavenly waters. As Shiva is identified with the Ganges river, Indra is also identified with rivers, particularly the Sarasvati.

Shiva is worshipped by the linga or standing stone. Indra and other Vedic Gods are worshipped by a pillar (*stambha*). The pillar and the linga are the same, symbols of the cosmic masculine force. Both Shiva and Indra represent the cosmic masculine force. Shiva's vehicle is a bull. Indra in the Vedas is frequently called a bull (*vrisha, vrishabha*). Shiva's bull is also identified with the rain cloud. Indra as the bull is lauded in the Vedas as the bringer of rain. The bull is also a symbol of the cosmic masculine force. OM, which is identified with both Indra and Shiva, is identified with a bull.

Shiva is identified with the Vedic deity Rudra, and most of the sacred chants to Shiva, like the Rudram from the Yajur Veda, are Vedic chants to Rudra. Vedic Rudra is identified in the Vedas with Indra. Both Indra and Rudra are deities of the middle region or the atmosphere (*Antarīksha*). Indra is the wielder of the thunderbolt, so is Rudra. The Vedic sons of Rudra are called the Maruts. The Maruts are the companions of Indra, who is their leader. Shiva travels with his host of Bhutas or ghosts. The Maruts are also spirits or Bhutas and in the Vedas they travel with Indra. Indra is the main deity of the Vedic rishis. Shiva is the main deity of the yogis. The yogis are usually rishis and vice versa. In fact, the Maruts, the sons of Rudra and the companions of Indra, are sometimes lauded as Brahmins, rishis or yogis.

Rudra-Shiva is propitiated to overcome death: so is Indra in the Vedas. There are Vedic prayers to protect us not only from the wrath of Rudra but also from the wrath of Indra. Both Rudra and Indra are propitiated to grant us fearlessness (*abhayam*) and for defeat of our enemies.

The early Upanishads identify Indra with Paramatman, the Supreme Self, just as the later Upanishads identify Shiva with Paramatman. Indra is called Prana or the life-force in the Upanishads. Shiva is also identified with Prana. The Maruts, the sons of Rudra-Shiva and the companions of Indra, are identified with the Pranas.

Shiva is a God of time, Kala. Indra is also a deity of time and eternity and rules the year in Vedic thought. Both Indra's and Shiva's role of destroying Prajapati or his son relate to their role as eternity (absolute time) destroying time or the year (relative time) represented by Prajapati and the sacrifice.

Indra is the deity who both rules and transcends the sacrifice, so is Shiva. Shiva, like Indra, is worshipped through the sacred fire. Shiva corresponds to the bhasma or the ashes left over from the sacred fire. Shaivite ascetics carefully attend their dhunis or sacred fires, which are built and tended to following Vedic practices. Hence Shaivism continues many Vedic rituals.

While Indra is predominant in the Rig Veda, in the Atharva and Yajur Vedas (which are also very old texts), Rudra is more prominent. Much of the symbolism of the Vedic sacrifice and the building of the fire altar relates to Rudra as well as to Indra. In the Shatapatha Brahmana for building up of the fire altar there are nine forms of Agni. Eight are names of Shiva and one is Kumara, the son of Shiva. Rudra like Indra is commonly identified with or associated with Agni, the deity of fire and the fire sacrifice.

The members of Shiva's family also have Vedic equivalents, which is a topic in itself, which will be mentioned only briefly. Skanda, the son of Shiva, is born of Agni or fire and is clearly identified with Agni. Agni in the Vedas is also called Kumara and Guha, which are names of Skanda. Ganesh is commonly lauded by a chant to Brihaspati from the Rig Veda (Gananam tva ganapatim), which correlates these deities.

Puranic Shiva and Vedic Indra share many common names and functions. A majority of the names and functions of one figure can be found in the other. Indra in the Vedas is called Shiva a number of times. Indra is also one of the names for Shiva in the thousand names of Shiva. The conclusion that we must draw from all this is that Indra and Shiva are essentially the same deity, according to a shift of language. The two deities are so close in function that they must have arisen from a common source and are part of a common tradition.

This does not mean that Indra and Shiva are identical. Vedic Indra and Puranic Shiva do not have the same appearance or identical stories. However, differences of forms do arise through time and do not require inventing a different tradition. The language of the Rudram, the most important chant to Shiva in the Vedas, is rather different than that of Puranic chants to Shiva, for example, but that does not mean that there are two different traditions, a Rudra tradition as opposed to a Shiva tradition.

The Hindu tradition has never been attached to mere names. Both Indra and Shiva have many names, as do other Vedic and Puranic deities. We moderns, however, are attached to names. We think that two different names must indicate two radically different things. This is only materialistic thinking and cannot comprehend the spiritual vision of the Vedas and Puranas. This type of name-oriented thinking is part of exclusivist religions which insist that there is only one true name for God, one true holy book and one true prophet or savior. Such thinking is contrary to the universalist Hindu vision which says that the Divine transcends all names and also contains all names and can never be limited to a single approach. Hence a name-oriented approach to Hindus traditions like the Vedic and the Shaivite has failed to understand the most basic principle of these teachings.

Only one basic and universal teaching can be found in India from early ancient times and characterizes the essence of the tradition. Vedic deities like Indra, Agni, Soma and Rudra are as freely identified with each other as are Puranic deities like Shiva, Vishnu and Devi (the Goddess). It shows no real understanding or appreciation of the tradition or of any of these deities to make them opposed to one another or to try to make one into the only true deity.

The Hindu approach has always allowed devotees to regard their form of the Divine as the supreme—whether Shiva, Vishnu, Devi or anything else. Yet at the same time it insists that devotees of one form allow devotees of another form to have the same freedom of view. The idea that there is only one God and his true name is Shiva, Vishnu, Allah, Christ or anything else, reflects exclusivist patterns of thought imported from non-Hindu religious beliefs and should not be applied to the Hindu tradition.

In truth there is no single deity called Indra or Shiva, or anything else. There is only the One Divine with innumerable names, forms and functions. The Indian spiritual tradition has generally formulated the supreme Divine as a deity of power, transcendence, independence and transformation. That is the basis of both Indra and Shiva.

Given the basic identity of Indra and Shiva there is no reason to propose a pre- or non-Vedic Shaivite religion in India. Shiva is present in Indra, as Indra takes another form through Shiva. There may have been other related teachings in ancient India that vary in details from what we know of in the few Vedic texts which have been preserved, like a Dravidian tradition of Shiva, Rudra or Indra worship. However, such teachings would be part of a greater tradition and not contrary traditions.

If Shiva and Indra are not two significantly different deities than all the ideas of a Vedic versus Shaivite, and Dravidian versus Aryan religions and cultures in India have no foundation to stand on, and much of modern scholarship on the Vedas and

Puranas has to be revised. On the other hand, the basic identity of Indra and Shiva eliminates many problems in interpreting the Indian spiritual tradition. There is no need to invent other traditions and outside influences, or mysterious and forgotten cultures, to explain the developments within Hinduism. All the main factors for such a development are found within the Vedic tradition itself.

An important point that should be emphasized is that Indra is the supreme deity of the Sarasvati culture as revealed in the Vedas. Shiva is the supreme deity of the Gangetic culture as revealed in the Puranas. Relative to the remains of ancient civilization in India, the Sarasvati sites (the Indus Valley sites) are definitely older. Hence the idea that Vedic Indra developed into Puranic Shiva appears to reflect the shift of culture in India when the Sarasvati went dry and the center of civilization shifted east to the Ganges.

Such changes in name and form must occur during the course of human history, particularly when there are great social and geological changes. Such a shift of culture in ancient India brought about the shift from Indra to Shiva. It was an organic transformation of the Vedic religion into the Puranic, not a radical break.

If we look deeply we see that the same basic spirit is present in both Indra and Shiva. Hence good devotees of Shiva should also be devotees of Indra and vice versa, or they may not understand the inner truth of their deity. Indra-Shiva is the basic deity of the Vedas and Puranas and of the Hindu tradition as a whole, which is not to exclude other important formulations of the Divine like Vishnu and the Devi but to show the continuity, creativity and universality of the tradition.

Hinduism and its branches like Shaivism are not ethnic teachings, they are universal. Nor is Shaivism a religion apart from Hinduism. Nor is Hinduism a composite of different religions including Shaivism. The Hindu trinity of Brahma, Vishnu and Shiva form an integral teaching and none of these deities excludes or denigrates the others. The Hindu tradition is a teaching not given relative to Dravidians only but for all humanity. The attempt to ethnicize Hinduism and divide it up into opposing doctrines has been part of an attempt of outside influences to dominate or convert the Hindus.

Dravidians have long been important contributors and supporters of all aspects of Hinduism or Sanatana Dharma. They have added many unique teachings of their own. But to think that Hinduism must be divided up into Dravidian and Aryan religions, which are fundamentally different from each other, in order to give the Dravidians credit for their accomplishments is an idea that only serves to divide up the tradition along questionable ethnic lines which serves no real purpose other than to destroy the universality of the teaching.

3.5
The Ancestry of Ravana

A close study of the Ramayana, particularly the last book or Uttara Kanda, reveals that Ravana, the enemy of Lord Rama, was not a Dravidian, as many people have thought, but related to the present peoples of Sri Lanka, who are considered to be Aryans—that Ravana was a migrant to Sri Lanka from the Vedic family of the Yadus, perhaps deriving originally from the city of Mathura south of Delhi. The first wave of migrants to Sri Lanka from the north was from Gujarat and of the Yadu family, which dominated the southwest of India and from the region of Gujarat had access to the sea on which they travelled far in their trading and colonizing ventures.

The Ramayana tells that Ravana, the king of Sri Lanka, had close connections with regions of the Yadus, which included Gujarat, parts of Maharashtra and Rajasthan up to Mathura south of Delhi. Ravana was related to Lavana, also regarded as a Rakshasa, of Madhupura (Mathura) in the region of the Surasenas, who was conquered by Rama's brother Shatrughna. After worshipping a Shiva Linga on the banks of the Narmada, in the more central Yadu region, Ravana was captured and held under the control of King Kartavirya Arjuna, one of the greatest Yadu kings. Later Ravana abducted Sita nearby on the banks of the Godavari, also in the south-eastern region of the Yadus. It appears that Ravana had territory in this Yadu region of India, reflecting his ancestral connections. In this same region Rama encountered Ravana's sister, who perhaps lived in this region, and that Ravana abducted Sita after Rama and Sita wandered unknowingly into his territory.

Ravana was known to be a Brahmin, a descendant of the Rishi Pulastya. Ravana was a great chanter of the Sama Veda, and a great devotee of Lord Shiva who had visited Mount Kailash, which he could have very well done from northern Yadu regions like Mathura. Ravana was well versed in Sanskrit and the composer of the famous Shiva Tandava Stotra. While one may argue that such a composition was of a later time than Ravana, it still shows a tradition that connects him with Sanskrit. His native tongue does not appear to have been Dravidian. He is portrayed as a migrant to Sri Lanka, which was not his original home, and captured the city of Sri Lanka from Kubera.

The Rama-Ravana story has similarities to the Deva-Asura conflict in ancient Hindu literature. In the original story found in the Puranas and Mahabharata there was a conflict between these two groups. The Devas or Suras had Brihaspati of the Angirasas as a guru, the Asuras, Daityas or Rakshasas had Shukra of the Bhrigus as their teacher. In other words both groups followed the Vedic religion, as the Angirasas and Bhrigus are the two main families of Vedic seers. The Devic culture, as described in the Manu Samhita, was centered on the Sarasvati region in north India. The Daitya (Asura) culture was located nearby in the region of the Bhrigus which was the southwest of India by the Arabian sea, as evidenced by the Bhrigu city Bhrigu-kaccha or Baruch, near modern Baroda. Varuna, the God of the sea, was the father of the Bhrigus, as the original Bhrigu was called Bhrigu Varuni. Gujarat was also the region of Sharyata Manava, one of the early sons of Manu, who founded the city of Kushasthali (later Dwaraka), who was similarly allied with the Bhrigus as his guru was Chyavana Bhargava, but whose kingdom was destroyed by the Asuras, who were perhaps these same

Daityas.

After a period of conflict the Deva and Asura groups forged an alliance. Yayati, the king in the line of Manu, had two wives. The first was Devayani, daughter of Shukra of the Bhrigus, the guru of the Daityas. The second was Sharmishtha, daughter of Vrisha Parvan, king of the Daityas. Thereby Yayati allied himself both with the Daitya kings and their gurus, bringing the blood lines of both Devas and Asuras and their gurus together. Yayati's youngest son Puru, born of Sharmishtha of the Asuras, inherited his central Sarasvati kingdom, which became the basis for many of the dynasties of later India including the Kurus, under whose patronage the Vedas were compiled, who therefore had Asuric blood in their veins. Yayati's oldest son Yadu, took over the region of the Daityas. The Yadus then became a very powerful military people, perhaps reflecting their Daitya connections. The Dravidians were regarded as descendants of Yayati's second son Turvasha, who was also a son of Devayani and in the line of the Bhrigus.

In this regard Rama's defeat of Ravana reflects other battles to subdue the Yadus, which are the main conflicts mentioned in Vedic and Puranic literature. These include Parashurama's defeat of the Yadus (Kartavirya Arjuna), Sagara of Ayodhya's defeat of the Yadus (the Haihayas), and Divodasa of Kashi's defeat of the Yadus (Vitihavya). The Yadus had the greatest and largest kingdoms of the Vedic people, and required keeping their prowess in check. Ravana was probably another militant Yadu similar to Kansa, the Yadu king of Mathura, who oppressed Krishna and his family. Yet the Yadus also produced many great sages, like Krishna and Ravana's own brother Vibhishana, and the other Aryan groups produced their share of evil men as well, like Duryodhana, the enemy of Arjuna, who was of the Kuru-Puru line.

The Dravidians, to the extent that we might be able to see the portrayal of different countries in the Ramayana, can be identified with Rama's companions like Hanuman and the region of Kishkindha (Karnataka), who at the time of Rama were under the domination of Ravana, through his alliance with their king Bali.

Previously scholars have not placed Aryan migrants into Sri Lanka before 600 BC. However the most recent scholarship reveals that Harappan and pre-Harappan cultures going back to 6000 BC in India were Vedic (note my book *Gods, Sages and Kings: Vedic Secrets of Ancient Civilization*: Motilal Banarsidass 1993), as they were based on the Sarasvati river of Vedic fame. Hence the date of their arrival into Sri Lanka may be pushed back much further. Harappan port cities like Lothal or Dholavira in Gujarat and Kutch have been found in the regions of the Yadus going back to the third millennium BC. These were probably the basis for the Yadu migration to Sri Lanka.

Sri Lankan Buddhists, such as predominate in the country today, traditionally held Ravana in respect, perhaps knowing he was one of their own ancestors. The famous Buddhist Sutra, the Lankavatara, looks to Sri Lanka as a holy land and the Sutra is given in honor of Ravana himself, who is styled as the king of the Yakshas, much like Kubera in Hindu thought.

Hence the recent tendency of South Indian politicians to look up to Ravana as a Dravidian hero may be misplaced. Ravana more properly belongs to the peoples of Sri Lanka, whose ancestry derives from the north, as does his brother Vibhishana who was an ally of Rama. Hanuman, who was Rama's best devotee, better represents the ancient Dravidians (who incidentally were also Aryans, in that they have always been portrayed in Vedic and Puranic literature as descendants of Vedic people, including the seers Agastya and Vishvamitra, and traditionally called themselves Aryans). Unfortunately various groups have tried to use the Ramayana for political gain without ever really examining the details of the story! Rama was not the first northerner to come to the south of India. The Yadus and Daityas had long before migrated to Sri Lanka. Rama came not as an intruder but as a liberator, freeing the south from the rule of Ravana and returning it to the rule of its own native peoples. Rama did not impose the rule of the north upon the south. For this reason he has always been traditionally worshipped in the south as a great hero. Such information requires a rewriting of Indian history, which is necessary on a number of accounts.

Section IV

Cultural Issues

4.1

East and West, Where is the Boundary?

The human mind has invented innumerable divisions, some of which help explain things in the world, others which create barriers that inhibit understanding. One of the most common divisions in culture is that of humanity into East and West. While this can be a convenient way to designate different types of cultures, particularly as the more materialistic or outward oriented West relative to the more spiritual and inward oriented East, it is not a rigid barrier. Taking it as a real boundary it can reinforce cultural prejudices and emphasize what may be only a temporary or partial distinction. We have often heard "East is east and West is west and never the twain shall meet." What does this division mean and how real is it?

We are all essentially human beings. Geographical, religious, political, cultural, and intellectual distinctions are secondary to the basic unity of human nature. We all have the same basic desires and fears, seeking of happiness, knowledge and security, and a mysterious longing for immortality. There is no human being who has ever lived who is not at the core, fundamentally akin to us.

Today we are entering into a global age and the barriers which have traditionally existed between people are gradually coming down all over the world. This we can observe as Western materialistic culture is moving to the East, and while Eastern spiritual culture is moving, at least to some degree, to the West. Even on a purely physical level we note that Asians are relocating to the West and constitute now a significant minority in Europe and America. Similarly a number of Europeans live or travel in Asia, and this trend is likely to grow in the future. The division of East and West, to the extent that it has been real, is disappearing and may eventually become a thing of the past.

We can observe that all the things Westerners have done, Easterners can do and, at least in individual cases, have done. Similarly all that Easterners have done, Westerners can do and, at least in individual cases, have also done. Easterners can be great scientists or technocrats. Indeed India is producing many of the best doctors, engineers and computer experts in the world. Westerners can take up the practice of Eastern yogic and meditational disciplines. As time goes on with the world-wide diffusion of ideas such phenomena will become more common.

The East-West division as we know it today was originally invented by so-called Westerners, the Europeans, particularly Western Europeans, as an expression of cultural superiority, particularly in the realm of science and technology. Everything to the East of them became the realm of the backward Easterners, whether it was such diverse groups as the Arabs, Hindus or Chinese. Eastern culture was defined in several ways. Generally it was regarded as mystical, unscientific, otherworldly, traditional, group oriented, and autocratic. This definition was relative to Western culture which defined itself as practical, scientific, this worldly, non-traditional, individual oriented, and democratic. Today the division has often been simplified with the materialistic West versus the spiritual East (though it would be more appropriate to regard all of the cultures of the world today as materialistic with the spiritual East being more the East of the past than the present).

What is Western culture and what constitutes it? Western or European culture has a base of Judeo-Christian religious and

Greco-Roman intellectual values, on a diversity of predominately Indo-European languages, peoples and their native beliefs. Out of this arose European art and culture, and the developments of modern science and technology. Western culture therefore is a polyglot affair, put together from different sources over time, and hardly a pure breed of any type.

The Western world looks back on two primary cultural eras, ancient Greece and the Renaissance. Both of these eras were creative because of an interchange of ideas with many outside sources. Renaissance thinkers studied Greek, Roman, Middle Eastern and sometimes Indian sources. The ancient Greeks and Romans took much from Egypt, Mesopotamia, Persia and India. These interchanges were not signs of the poverty of their culture but its openness. Yet besides these two great cultural eras the religious era of the early Christianity overshadows them in the Western mind. The religious movement of Christianity was exclusive, not synthetic, and covers over the otherwise more syncretic nature of Western culture.

Western culture is generally defined in two ways, which are usually combined, though they are contradictory. First it is regarded as scientific and rational, as opposed to oriental culture which is unscientific and mystical. Second by its Christian religion (with which Judaism and Islam may be combined), it is regarded as humanitarian and monotheistic, while Eastern religions are viewed as otherworldly and polytheistic or monistic.

That the Christian religious tradition is not necessarily scientific or rational is well known to everyone. The ongoing battle between science and religion, or church and state in the West, cannot be missed by any thoughtful person. The rejection of the authority of the Church was necessary for the development of science in the first place. Many Western religious groups today still promote a literal Biblical idea of creation that the world is only six thousand years old, which is a total denial of the evidence of science. On the other hand, the Hindu and Buddhist account of the origin of the universe, with multi-billion year cycles of creation and destruction, is much more in harmony with modern science, though these Eastern religions were not originally looked to as anything rational by the Western mind.

The Western scientific background moreover originates from the pre-Christian Greeks. Yet in terms of religion the ancient Greeks—as all the pre-Christian peoples of Europe—had a religion like the oriental or the Hindu and were Pagans. They used images, practiced temple worship, maintained a sacred fire and often had Gods of the same name and function as the Hindu. Similarly the accusations of polytheism and idolatry made against oriental religions like Hinduism and Buddhism, are the same as those made against the Pagan Europeans from whom science and rationality first arose. In time Christianity (and Islam as well) adapted the Pagan philosophies of the Greeks (Plato and Aristotle), along with Greek medicine, science and other cultural factors, as it had no real philosophy or science, no real intellectual culture of its own.

On the other hand, Oriental cultures, like India, have had their own traditions of rational philosophy much like the Greeks, as we can see in the Upanishads, Sankhya, Nyaya-Vaisheshika, and the Buddhist schools, which similarly emphasize reason and dialectic but combined with ethical and meditational disciplines. In fact Greek philosophy like Plato or Parmenides has many affinities with the Hindu. Similarly Greek medicine and astronomy has much in common with Ayurvedic medicine and the astronomical systems of India.

The philosophical and religious background from which science emerged via the Greeks therefore has more in common with the oriental religions and with the Hindu and the Buddhist than the Judeo-Christian tradition. We can see this today wherein many scientists have found a common chord in different strands of oriental mysticism. Therefore there is no reason to associate Western science with predominant Western religions. The basis for Western science lies in the free inquiry of the Greeks, which was also represented by their religion that has much depth yet to be explored, as Greek mythology so clearly indicates. The Hindus have a similar mythic tradition that is yet more profound than the Greek as it is more concerned with the yogic quest.

Moreover, oriental mysticism is not necessarily unscientific or irrational. It is part of an entire science of Yoga that is laid out as systematically as any modern science. Hindu and Buddhist spiritual teachings are not filled with dogma and superstition, but with various methods of inquiry and experiments in consciousness. This has attracted many Westerners to them, not in denial of rationality, but often as an extension of it to a spiritual level. Hence the Oriental and the Pagan is the mother not only of mysticism but of science and philosophy. What later Western religions brought was mainly dogma and fundamentalism, not any internal science of mysticism or any external physical science.

Therefore to say that scientific Westerners should not adapt Eastern spirituality does not make any sense. The criticisms of Eastern spirituality as being unsuitable for Westerners are more appropriate for Christianity and related religions, which tend to be anti-rational, than for Hinduism and Buddhism, which are rational approaches to the spiritual life. If we are mean that as rational people we need a rational system of spirituality, that would align us with the so-called Eastern religions, as well as the mysticism of the ancient Greeks and Romans. If we are saying that as rational people all religion should be rejected as irrational, we should recognize that Eastern religions like Hinduism and Buddhism are not irrational or emotional belief systems, but ways of clearing the mind of preconceptions and prejudice for the direct perception of Truth.

Other people say that since Western culture is individualistic Westerners should not follow Eastern culture because it is traditional and authoritarian and denies the freedom that is the real spirit of Western culture. However Hindu thought is the most individualistic in the world. It teaches that the individual, that you yourself are God or the Divine power behind the universe. It does not subordinate the conscious individual to any authority or belief but emphasizes that we must be true to our own deepest nature, that the highest truth is to be who we really are apart from all external conditioning influences. Freedom or Moksha is the very goal of Hindu thought, but this is not freedom within the field of time (which being limited is the realm of bondage) but freedom to transcend time.

Western tends to mean modern, as Eastern tends to mean ancient. However in a hundred years, India or China could be at the forefront of technology or what we now call Western civilization. In the thirteenth century the Chinese had gunpowder and the compass, the basis of modern technology, and the Europeans were technologically primitive. Such temporal distinctions are seldom enduring.

Yet by Western culture today neither Western religions nor Western intellectual culture is usually meant. It is Western popular or commercial culture: rock music, movies, television, fast food, and so on. Western pop culture is more of an anti-culture than a true culture. It not only destroys the culture of the countries it invades, it has already undermined whatever culture (that is, ethical or aesthetic refinement) that was in Western culture to begin with. Most of so-called Western art is a thing of the past, with little great art added since the advent of modern mass technological culture which occurred after the first World War.

Hence when Westerners insist upon maintaining the purity of Western culture what do they mean? Do they mean upholding Christianity? Do they mean upholding Greco-Roman or European intellectual values? Do they mean upholding modern Western pop culture or Western business interests? Is there a cultural purity or homogeneity in any of this? And what do so-called progressive Easterners mean when they speak of bringing in the benefits of Western culture? Apart from technological expertise, the West has very little culture to offer.

Most interestingly, we note that the division between East and West is often made into a one way street. In America we are told, particularly by our religious leaders, that we should not adopt Eastern spiritual or religious teachings because they are foreign and "Eastern" and not appropriate for we "Westerners," who should follow a Western religion or spiritual path. However Western religious groups don't hesitate to try to convert the people of Asia, which has always been one of their primary goals. Western missionaries don't tell Easterners that their "Western" Christian religion is not appropriate for the people of Asia who should follow an "Eastern" religion more in harmony with their cultural background, like Hinduism or Buddhism. Western religious leaders treat their Western religions as of global relevance, but they do not like it if people of Eastern religious backgrounds consider that their religions also possess a global significance. This is an obvious cultural prejudice. Is not religion meant to deal with what is universal anyway?

If Western religious groups really believe in the division of East and West, the first thing for them to do would be to stop trying to convert the people of Asia. What they believe in is not that there is a rigid division between East and West, but that the East should be Westernized. In fact Western religions in Asia are usually not promoting the scientific, rational or progressive side of Western culture, but imposing on the East the irrational, unscientific and unspiritual part of Western religions that is being rejected in the Western world, and which will only serve to keep the people of Asia backward and bound by medieval superstitions.

Japan has become a modern Asian culture that can compete with the West in terms of science and business by adapting its own Buddhist and Shinto traditions to the conditions of the modern world, not by becoming Christian or Islamic. The Philippines, on the other hand, perhaps the most staunch Christian nation of Asia, remains among the most backward. Hence it is not Western religion that is benefiting Asia, but the confidence of the people of Asia in themselves and their own traditions and their ability to adapt them to the changed circumstances of the modern world.

While Western culture is exporting itself to Asia, the division of East and West is used to prevent Eastern culture from being imported in to the West. However, if Western culture is going to be exported to Asia, Eastern culture must come to the West. The trade of ideas and culture can no more be a one way street than the trade of merchandise. If the East can benefit from Western culture, then certainly the division between East and West is not real. Then the West can benefit from Eastern culture without people losing their real nature, which after all is a matter of the heart, not of geographical divisions.

And we should ask, where is this mythical boundary between East and West located? Is Eastern Europe of the East because it is "Eastern" or the West because it is European? Is the so-called Near East part of Eastern culture or of the West because much of it is equivalent in longitude with parts of Europe? What about Africa or South America, which are on the same longitude with Europe and North America, the bastions of the so-called West? They have older cultures which resemble the Eastern or Asiatic more so than the Western or European. Are the American Indians Easterners or Westerners? Their culture and racial type is more of the Asiatic, yet they are the native people of a region regarded as Western.

On what basis do we make the distinction of East and West? If it is by race, we must remember that many of the people of Asia—like those of India and the Middle East—are of the same Caucasian race as the people of Europe. If it is by color of skin we should note that the northern Chinese have a white skin color like the Europeans. If it is by language, we must note that most of the languages of India and Iran are of the same Indo-European family as those of Europe, whereas those of the Near East are of different families like the Semitic. By the logic of language India would belong to the West and Saudi Arabia to the East. If it is by religion, there are a number of Christians and Muslims in Southeast Asia. Are they Easterners or Westerners? Muslims share the same general Biblical religious background as the Christians. Are they therefore Westerners? Would we therefore call Cairo in Egypt a Western city? And what of the many Americans and Europeans who are embracing Hindu, Buddhist and Taoist practices? Are they thereby ceasing to be Westerners?

If the division of East and West is by technological advance, then Japan belongs to the West and as various Asian countries develop economically then we would have to say that they have joined the Western world, even if they may have preserved their older Eastern religious practices. Similarly Mexico and other Latin American countries as well as Eastern Europe by their poverty would have to be Eastern. If economic affluence makes the division between East and West then in medieval times when China and India were affluent and Europe was poor, was Europe then of the East and Asia of the West?

The Chinese were originally suspicious of Buddhism because coming from India to the West, it was considered to be a Western religion. In embracing Buddhism did they become Westerners? The Romans regarded Christianity as an Eastern religion and were similarly suspicious of it. Did Christianity turn them into Easterners? On the other hand, the pre-Christian Greek, Roman and European religions had deities and practices and a social culture very close to the ancient Hindu Vedic, as is evident from abundant similarities of language and customs. Would we say therefore that the ancient Europeans were originally Easterners like the Hindus but became Westerners through the adaptation of Christianity, another Eastern religion?

Westerners have designated the majority of the world to be Eastern. It appears that whatever seems different than the North

American and Western European can fall under the label Eastern. Yet such cultures as India and China—which are lumped together as Eastern—are as distinct from one another as each is from the culture of Europe. All these so-called Easterners are not alike. They are a far more heterogenous group than so-called Westerners. The Muslims are said to be Easterners, yet they come from the same religious background as Western culture and their Koran is based upon the Bible. They also use Greek philosophy and medicine as have the Christians. We could argue from their cultural and religious forms that the Muslims and Europeans are both Westerners. Certainly the Hindus see their religions in the same light. Westerners should stop lumping India, China and the Middle East in this negative category of the East, which is mainly a way of dismissing what happens in these countries as irrelevant. Westerners must learn to deal with each of these cultures as they are, which is quite different, not just generically Eastern.

The division of East and West is generally a one-sided affair, a barrier protecting Europe and North America from outside influences, particularly those of religion, while they spread their culture all over the world. However, we don't reject a peach because its original home in China makes it an Eastern fruit. So too, knowledge and culture are things that are universal. And many aspects of our culture today have come from quite diverse places throughout the world. Just as Europe and America are having a strong cultural and religious effect on Asia, so India, Japan, China and other Asiatic countries are affecting Western cultural and religious views in ways the West may not yet suspect. In fact the essence of culture lies in broadening one's cultural base to include as much of human culture as possible. This is what is regarded as being cosmopolitan rather than provincial.

Just as we all use different food items that have been developed throughout different parts of the world, so have different cultures and sciences developed in various lands. We should use each of these for its objective worth and not be disturbed by differences of names. Nor will we find that only our culture is valuable. We will discover something of value in each culture. We are all human beings and all human culture belongs to each of us. Whatever any human culture has produced is part of our own humanity. The racial, linguistic, religious and cultural divisions between people should not be taken rigidly. They are the different facets of the same gem of our common humanity. Like the different petals of a flower each has its unique place and beauty but this need not serve to make them hostile or alien to each other. This does not mean that all cultures are simply the same or equal, but that they are all part of a greater human culture which we all must discover.

What does the East have to offer the West? It is obviously a much older, better developed, wiser and more tolerant, as well as more scientific approach to the spiritual life. Similarly the West has to offer the East a more scientific, and often more humane and practical way to organize the outer life. Those of us who are Westerners may have to humble ourselves a little to recognize what the East has to offer, but we must face the facts. If we really want to grow as a planet we must take the best from all cultures. When Westerners refuse to examine Eastern spiritual teachings because it may cause them to lose their assumed Western identity, they are only cutting off a part of their greater and deeper humanity.

If Westerners really want to help the people of Asia they should teach them practical and humanitarian ways to organize their societies. When they try to convert them to Western religions they are doing both them and themselves a disservice because religion is what the East already has, and what the West needs to seek from it.

Such Asian cultures as India and Tibet did develop a greater knowledge of consciousness or the internal world, just as Europe and America developed a greater consciousness of the external world. Westerners need not feel culturally denigrated by benefitting from the wisdom of India any more than Hindus have to feel debased by taking on the benefits of technology from Europe and America. Just as the people of Asia must adapt technology to their own environment, so must those in America must adapt this oriental science of consciousness to their own lives. It is an issue of human growth, not of the advancement of one geographical region only.

Naturally it is hard to understand foreign cultures, just as the sounds of a foreign language will not at first make sense. It is easier to see the faults rather than the merits in one's neighbors. If we look to the differences we will find them but if we look to the unity that is also there. It depends on where we place our attention and what we value in life.

Our real goal as a species should be to create a common spiritual and sacred culture which is beyond mere geographical divisions, whatever they may be. "All the world is one family," is a great statement from the Vedic tradition, which tradition therefore belongs to all of us. The challenge today is to create a global culture. This is to recognize our common human heritage in all culture and to anchor that culture to spiritual values, the pursuit of Self-realization as the real goal of humanity.

4.2

The Value of Hindu Culture for the World

To find truth, all the great sages have told us that one must go beyond all outer divisions of race, creed, caste, nationality or culture. Only those who can step beyond the outer identities that divide human beings can arrive at the one source of all things—the true Self of all beyond time, space and circumstance.

This, however, does not mean that culture has no purpose or value in the spiritual life. Many of the same sages were also great founders, upholders or reformers of culture. Many left not only works on spiritual knowledge but those on the arts and sciences, and social and political issues. This in fact was the tradition of the Vedic seers, who first established Hindu culture in ancient times. They were said to be "*bhūtakrit*," world-makers or establishers of culture and custom.

If we look at humanity through history we can observe that men and women of spiritual realization have not come equally from all cultures, which would be the case if culture were merely a neutral factor in the spiritual life. Some cultures, particularly India, have created an environment that has better allowed for great spiritual personages to arise. There has been an ongoing stream of great spiritual figures in India since the ancient Vedic sages to modern times. Even the modern teacher who has gone furthest to negate cultural and religious identities as relevant to the spiritual life, J. Krishnamurti, not surprisingly came from the

Brahmin culture of India.

Other cultures, particularly those of the European and the Islamic world, have rarely produced comparable spiritual figures and have not given them much value, when they have arisen within their ranks. They still trumpet their one son of God or one prophet as if only one great religious figure were possible, which becomes the sad epitaph on the spirituality of their culture. Emphasizing only one such figure prevents others from developing or from being recognized should they arise. The concept of a person of spiritual realization—a human being who has realized the Divine or Truth in his or her own consciousness and has thereby transcended all time and space—is not formally recognized by their cultures at all; in fact it is regarded as heresy or delusion.

The Indic traditions recognize that Truth can be found through many different sages, and must ultimately be realized by each individual in his or her own right, while these exclusivist approaches recognize only one great being who existed at one time, and require that all other people look to that one person and his authoritative revelation for establishing their relationship with God. Such a negative attitude about the human capacity for spiritual knowledge must have an effect in stultifying the spiritual potential of the culture itself.

Even the Buddhist cultures of the East, though they have the concept of an enlightened sage, have not produced the great stream of sages that has come out of India, though they have produced a number of such remarkable figures. This is perhaps because their cultures as a whole are less spiritually oriented and more practically minded than the Hindu. Therefore we must conclude that culture can be important and that the culture of India, even with its many inadequacies, has given the world a better basis for the spiritual life than those of other countries. While the deficiencies in Indian culture today are more visible to the outward eye, like the overpopulation or lack of sanitation, this should not detract us from appreciating India's inner and historically more enduring qualities. Nor should it prevent us from extracting the higher values of Indian culture from its lower forms and implementing them in our own lives, using them to fill the growing spiritual deficiencies in cultures throughout the world.

If we look at India over the last hundred years we see a stream of great spiritual personages including Ramakrishna, Vivekananda, Rama Tirtha, Aurobindo, Ramana Maharshi, Anandamayi Ma, Shivananda, Neem Karoli Baba, and Nityananda—to mention a few—and all great individuals, not the products of any school or organization, and not clones of one another. If we look at the West or the Islamic world over the last thousand years, it is difficult to find such a number of people of spiritual realization. Without a cultural support such a great assembly could not arise or would not be appreciated. While these sages are the fruit, the culture is the field that nourishes the trees (teachings) on which they grow.

However, Hindu teachers in the West have brought with them very little of Hindu culture. They have not wanted to impose their culture on Westerners, who might not appreciate it. They have been under the impression that some Hindu practices, like the worship of images, would be looked at unfavorably by Westerners with their aniconic religious backgrounds, and therefore used as a pretext for rejecting the rest of their teaching. Hence they have stressed yogic and meditational practices and have even encouraged Westerners to maintain their own cultural and religious identities, though these might be opposed to the deeper practices they are teaching.

The worship of the Gods and Goddesses, Hindu devotional meditations, pujas and rituals are little known or understood in the West. Many Western followers of Hindu Yoga have never entered a Hindu temple or seen a puja performed, except as a curiosity. Ayurveda, the Vedic medical system, is only now getting some recognition in the West. Vedic astrology is just beginning to surface and looks like it also will become quite popular, at least in astrological circles. Hindu music has made a mark of its own. Sanskrit poetry, drama and aesthetics, the most extensive, intricate, profound and spiritual in the world, is little known or appreciated. Even the poets of the Western world who aim at a symbolic or mystical approach do not have an idea as to how extensively this realm has already been explored in India with such figures as Kalidas. The Vedas and Upanishads, the great source teaching behind these numerous currents, are largely unknown, even by name, by those who practice or teach Yoga!

Perhaps this hiding of Hindu cultural forms, which occurred among the educated in India as well, was necessary at the turn of the last century when the West was still dominated by Christianity, but it is no longer true and is becoming counter-productive as Westerners are looking for new religious forms, for example, a religion of the Divine Mother such as Hinduism has much more clearly articulated than the predominant Western religions. Other spiritual traditions have not kept their cultures so much in the background in their coming to the West. Chinese and far Eastern culture, Chinese medicine, Chinese astrology (I Ching), martial arts, Japanese poetry (haiku), and Chinese and Japanese painting are as well known as the meditation tradition (Chan or Zen). Much of the popularity of Tibetan Buddhism has come from the pujas, visualizations and devotional meditations they teach their followers, along with Tibetan chants.

An American Yoga teacher and friend of mine, who also studies Tibetan Buddhism, told me once that he was given a great new secret and powerful meditation teaching from a Lama, unlike anything he had gotten from his Yoga teacher, who stressed Hatha Yoga, though he had lived and studied with him four years in India. This practice was meditating on a Tibetan deity and doing a puja to it. When I told him that such puja and devotional meditation was the main practice of Hinduism and was much more developed in the Hindu tradition than the Buddhist, which had largely adopted it from the Hindu, he was shocked. Why had he not heard of this from his own teacher? When he had asked for religious instruction from his Hindu teacher, he was told to stick to Christian approaches, which was particularly disturbing to him as his own religious background was Jewish!

The point of all this is that culture is not necessarily a detriment to the spread of spiritual knowledge, any more than it is a detriment to its arising. Nor is Indian culture anything to hide or be ashamed of. It is not something contrary to or apart from yogic spirituality but the unfoldment of meditative values in the outer life. It is not something inferior to Western culture that one should be ashamed of, but a vastly superior system and a potential means of uplifting Western culture. Though perhaps technologically deficient compared to that of the West, in the spiritual, philosophical and aesthetic realms Hindu culture goes far beyond it.

Modern Hindus in India tend to be apologetic about their culture, and its many temples, rituals, chants, festivals, forms and images. If they have a spiritual side they are more likely to connect with Vedantic ideas or with modern teachers like Krishnamurti or Rajneesh, where there appears to be little concern or even a disdain for this plethora of forms. They may prefer Western intellectual culture, which appears more sophisticated. They are also suffering from a misunderstanding of the beauty and importance of their culture, though it must be admitted that much of Hindu culture today is in decay. This, however, should not be a pretext for abandoning it in favor of a spiritually inferior culture, but for reviving it. Once we understand the importance of culture in the spiritual life, we begin to appreciate what Hinduism has been all about. The spiritual path is Rama but a spiritual culture is Sita. Rama must win and save Sita or he cannot fulfill his destiny.

Hindus need to awaken to the importance of their spiritual tradition including not only its great formless teachings like Vedanta, but its beauty of spiritual culture, particularly its culture of devotion (*bhakti*), which is one of the most sublime and exalted cultures the world has ever produced. They need to recognize the importance of their spiritual culture for all humanity, which is spiritually starved and generally deprived of any deeper cultural nourishment. Individuals in the West who have true spiritual aspiration often fail to go far because there is nothing in their culture that supports them. Most of the rest of the world is confined in the sterility of a materialistic and intellectual culture, or that of dogmatic and exclusive religions, either of which is a desert for the soul. Without the waters of a true spiritual culture the soul of humanity is likely to remain barren.

Hindus need to stop dividing their culture from its higher spiritual traditions. There is no conflict between Vedantic philosophy and Hindu ritualistic and devotional forms. In fact it is the latter that have provided the ground in which the former is able to grow. Hindus should no longer deny the integrality of yogic spirituality and Hindu culture, but rather show it as a model for the integration of Yoga into other cultures.

This does not mean that Hindus should try to impose their cultural forms on others, which is not their tendency anyway, but they should share them and allow others to use them. For this Hindus must uphold the value of Hindu culture in their own lives and in India itself. This is not to encourage a mere superficial Hindu pride or Hindu cultural elitism. It is to stop the process of devaluing this great culture, which alone of the world's cultures appears to really support the complete unfoldment of the spirit or inner Self.

While spiritually advanced individuals may have little need for any culture or outward forms, the world as a whole needs a broad creative and spiritual culture to nourish the diversity of human temperaments. It is not enough to teach people the value of meditation and otherwise educate them along scientific, intellectual or technological lines, or place them back in their own religious and cultural backgrounds which are inimical to the spiritual quest. This is not transcendence of culture. It is an acquiescence to non-spiritual or materialistic cultural values which prevent the spiritual life from truly flowering.

The majority of people find an easier access to the spiritual life if they first are exposed to a spiritual culture: for example, a spiritualized philosophy, poetry, art, music, medicine or astrology. We need a broad field (*Prakriti*) of cultural growth in order to allow the widest and most diverse set of approaches to the spirit (*Purusha*). Individuals are so different that the example of any one teacher or spiritual path is not enough. Hence the linking of the spiritual life to all aspects of life and culture is essential. While a rare individual can go directly to Truth (pure consciousness), cultures need to explore the domains of the mind: art, philosophy, medicine, and science. While the evolution of the individual can follow a vertical ascent, culture moves more slowly, expanding horizontally before being able to rise to a new level vertically.

The forms of Hindu culture are among the most spiritually oriented in the world. They can serve as a basis for the forms of a new spiritual world culture. Such domains of culture directed toward the spiritual quest as poetry, philosophy and mythology have had their greatest development in India. It is not just Yoga, meditation and renunciation of the world that India has to offer but the abundant forms of a spiritual culture. Naturally these cultural forms will have to be modified, adapted and purified to some degree relative to time and place. There are aspects of them that have become rigid or corrupt. Most of the aspects of Hindu culture that are objected to in the West, like the hereditary caste system, are not in harmony with their original meaning anyway. To defend Hindu culture is to return to its purer and more spiritual form. It does not require hiding its present inadequacies. All the world's cultures need such reform and renovation. It is not denying one's culture to do this but affirming its creative capacity.

Naturally those who have other cultural preferences may object to any apparent glorification of Hindu culture. They would prefer if Hindu culture would stay hidden and lacking in confidence so that they can spread their own cultural forms upon the world without competition from India. Western culture, whether atheist, Christian or Islamic, is still trying to impose its cultural forms as superior in India itself. And Hindu culture does not make an adequate effort to defend itself from such assaults. The point is not to simply defend India or Hindu culture but to uphold the higher spiritual values which are more present within it than other cultures, particularly that of the unspiritual West. It is not a national or cultural but ultimately spiritual issue, concerning not just India but all humanity.

There are those who do not like the term "Hindu culture" and would prefer the more general term "Indian culture." To them the term Hindu connotes a religious limitation but Indian is more embracing of the diverse culture of the subcontinent. However the culture of India is primarily Hindu and Sanskritic. Even the Buddhists, Jains and Sikhs, and to some extent the Muslims and Christians of India, have followed a Hindu or Sanskritic type culture.

The music of India is Hindustani, based upon Hindu and Sanskrit works going back to the Sama Veda. The dance is based upon Hindu temple dance. The native medicine, Ayurveda, is rooted in the Vedas themselves, as is the astrology, Jyotish. The poetry and drama traditions revolves around Hindu mythology. The exercise tradition of Hatha Yoga is rooted in the religious sadhana tradition. The literature and philosophy all looks back to Sanskrit, which derives from the Vedas. The spirit and forms of the religion permeate all aspects of Indian culture, far more than Christianity permeates the culture of Europe which contains considerable pre-Christian Greco-Roman and post-Christian Western intellectual influences.

Unfortunately many modern Hindus are rushing to embrace a superficial Western culture, imitating its more mundane forms of thought and expression. This may be a great loss not only for India but for the whole world. There are enough people in the world exploring mass media culture, writing superficially about political affairs or common human emotions. There are enough students studying Western philosophy and art. How many educated Hindus know Shakespeare and how many know Kalidas and Bhartrihari, Indian poets and men of spiritual realization whose knowledge of consciousness dwarfed not only that of Shakespeare but that of Einstein? Why aren't there Kalidas festivals in India comparable to the Shakespeare festivals in England and other English speaking countries?

Why should the youth of India focus their studies on Western thinkers while much greater figures in the culture of India are ignored throughout the world? Why should they emulate such thinkers as Marx, Kant or Freud, when they have those from Shankara to Sri Aurobindo, who could contain the entire minds of all these Western thinkers in one corner of their much vaster awareness? India's place is to pour forth the glory of the spirit through every cultural form. It should not merely conserve but also renew and expand its great spiritual cultural heritage, and allow the rest of the world to benefit from it. For this Hindus must show their dedication to Hindu culture, not as a form of national culture but as a form of world culture. To do this they must be willing to express their culture to the world, not as cultural propaganda but as the gift of the heart. This does not mean that Hindus should not use computers or other technological advances but that they should use them to develop their own spiritual culture, not to adapt a less evolved Western civilization.

Today there is little real culture left in the world anywhere. Modern pop consumer culture is taking over in every country, except where fundamentalist religion holds on with its rigid and sterile forms. Western intellectual and artistic culture has been in decline for several decades. Yet this cultural vacuum is a great opportunity for a spiritual culture, such as that of India, to move in. However for this to occur Hindus must awaken to their mission and look at their heritage in its universal relevance. This is one of the most important endeavors of the coming century. Perhaps as Westerners like myself come to appreciate Hindu culture, which is like the grace of the Divine Mother, Hindus themselves will begin to recognize their heritage and once more use it in a creative and beneficial way for all.

4.3

An American Discovers the Vedas

Why would an American dedicate himself to studying the ancient Vedas of India? And how could an American, coming from a totally different cultural background, find deep affinity with the Vedic teachings, which most Hindus today themselves can't even relate to? How did such a person get started in studying the Vedas? In the modern world everyone, including Hindus, appears to be trying to adopt Western culture with its scientific and technological advances and economic affluence. Why would a person go in the other direction and look to the East, particularly when it was not a matter of academic study, nor did it promise any material reward?

As I have written many books and articles on the Vedas and travelled through America and India over the past few years promoting Vedic knowledge, I am often asked such questions, particularly by Hindus in India or Indo-Americans, who usually do not have the time and are lacking in the motivation to examine their own tradition. Confronted with an American dedicated to the Vedas, Hindus find me not only to be an anomaly but also a question mark on what they themselves are doing. Sometimes they find it an inspiration to reexamine their own roots.

This is a difficult query for me to answer. I will begin by relating something of my life. There is really nothing in my family or educational background that would explain my connection with the Vedas or even India. I was the second in a family of ten children, born in a small city in Wisconsin in the Midwest in 1950. Both my parents came from strict Catholic backgrounds, my father of Irish ancestry and my mother German, and both were raised on dairy farms. One of my uncles was a priest and a missionary to South America (which example my mother wanted me to follow). My parents did not have any extensive education. My mother did not even attend high school. My father went to college only briefly, not completing a single year, and served in the army during World War II. Though both my parents were open minded they never oriented me in the direction of India or anything mystical. Yet my mother in particular did encourage a religious attitude in me according to her Catholic background.

I myself went to Catholic school until the fifth grade (age ten). We were taught to look on Protestants with suspicion. Asia was like another world, a land of backward, primitive people needing conversion, and we were taught that Asian religions like Hinduism or Buddhism were pagan, if not demonic. After much moving of our residence from city to city, and from state to state, as my father was a realtor, we finally settled down in Denver, Colorado in the Rocky Mountain region. There, owing to the financial burden of so many children, we switched to public school which brought us out of the shell of Catholic beliefs, and first exposed me seriously to the realm of science, which I found much more appealing and expansive to my mind than the church. Yet public schools had no real mention of India either, except as a big country in Asia suffering from poverty, overpopulation, and social backwardness.

I had an inquisitive mind as a child and began developing my own studies outside of school. I had an interest in geography since seven or eight years of age and became aware that there was much more to the world than America. Foreign lands of all types fascinated me, particularly Europe. I began reading various books starting with science and history around the age of eleven, which broadened my view of life and caused me to question my Catholic upbringing. I found the ideas of modern astronomy, like the vastness of the universe and the relativity of time and space, to be much more intriguing than Catholic views of creation that seemed rather artificial and stultified.

I left the Catholic church of my own accord about the age of fourteen. This came not only from the clash between the church and science, but from having read history and discovering that the church often stood for political oppression and social exploitation, not anything truly holy. I studied the history of the popes and began to see that religious institutions were more political establishments than real spiritual centers. I felt that if there was a God, it was an impersonal reality, not a personal God with his own whims, judgements and partialities, his chosen people and his special church such as I was taught. Yet though I left the church, I still felt that there was a spiritual reality in life, which I found in nature, particularly in the high mountains which I loved. This spiritual reality I felt was an inner experience quite divorced from churches and creeds.

By the time of high school my own studies were of more interest to me than the classes I was taking in school. I had an intellectual awakening about the age of sixteen which caused me to study European literature, particularly symbolic poets, existential philosophers and psychologists like Freud and Jung. I felt that American culture was very superficial compared to the European. Yet examining the mystical and poetic sides of the European mind, I also eventually found them to be lacking. I saw that the great intellectuals and artists of the West, the geniuses who were regarded as the highest human types, were still plagued with doubt, depression and uncertainty, often took drugs, or even went insane, or committed suicide. They obviously had not found any lasting peace or ultimate truth.

About the same time that I began examining European

thought, as a secondary interest I began examining the Eastern spiritual traditions of Hinduism, Buddhism and Taoism. Some of this came as part of the late sixties counterculture movement, which included a fascination with Eastern gurus, but most of it was the product of my own independent and more philosophical search. Between these different Eastern teachings I found a common truth—consciousness as the supreme reality and meditation as the way to realize it. Yet it was among the teachings of Yoga and Vedanta that I found the views which most resonated with my inner being, particularly the sense of the supreme Self (Atman) and pure Existence (Brahman) as the highest truth. For example, I remember walking home from high school one day and looking up at the blue sky and realizing that it was the presence of Krishna, who represented the cosmic power of bliss. This experience occurred before I encountered the Hare Krishna movement and was not produced by any evident outer influences.

After high school I attended a local college briefly, in which I found little to interest me. I remember taking a class on Cosmology and Metaphysics, which was actually in the graduate studies department though I was a freshman. I thought the class might have something mystical in it. Instead I discovered that it was mainly a science class, with a few cosmological speculations thrown in, generally of a materialistic nature. The teacher could not even decide whether there was any God or spiritual reality to the universe or not. This caused me to feel that the academic world had no capacity to answer the real questions of life. Hence I abandoned college after completing less than a semester.

About this time I also came into contact with local spiritual teachers and Yoga groups in Denver, through which I learned of various gurus and practices, including Yoga and meditation, which I began to do on a regular basis. A couple of years later I travelled to California and visited many of the spiritual groups there. However I never really connected with the spiritual groups based in America. I had more interest in India itself and teachings that were more traditional. I had a serious bent of mind and did not feel satisfied with American groups which were largely social movements or cults centered around one person, in which one's personal relationship with the teacher generally outweighed any real interest in spiritual studies, which often did not go very far. I have always distrusted mass movements and fads of all types, including the pop spirituality that has developed in the West.

I came to learn of the teachings of great modern Hindu gurus of India most notably Ramakrishna, Ramana Maharshi, Anandamayi Ma, and Sri Aurobindo. In these teachers and their teachings I felt something truly solid and real. As several of these figures had already passed away, I wrote to their centers in India and developed contact with some of their living disciples. Most notably I corresponded with Anandamayi Ma for several years, who was still alive at the time. But more so than any particular teacher the Vedantic teaching interested me, particularly the Upanishads, which appeared as the ideal combination of spiritual philosophy and mystical poetry. I felt in them the core teaching that I was looking for in all spiritual teachings.

This led me to the works of Shankaracharya, the great commentator on the Upanishads according to the system of Advaita Vedanta. The Advaitic view of the pure unity of truth and the illusory nature of the world, agreed with my experience of life through the political and social turbulence of the late sixties and early seventies. Yet I was also drawn towards the earlier Vedas and their mysterious mantras, with which most Vedantic teachers have little concern. I had a sense of things ancient and wanted to know the earliest teachings of humanity. The idea of the ancient rishis and seers appealed to me and I wanted to know who they were.

I also had a poetic bent of mind and wrote poetry of a mystical and symbolic type since the time I was sixteen. I used images of the dawn and the night, fire, the wind, and the sun, along with gods and goddesses, with the forces of nature appearing as powers of both the human and cosmic mind in their interplay. Later I found that these same images predominated in the Vedas themselves.

Of the great modern yogis, Sri Aurobindo was the greatest poet, and so naturally his work had an appeal to me. The beginning of the chapters in his book *The Life Divine* contained various Vedic quotes, particularly from the Rig Veda, which I found to be particularly inspiring. I noted in a list of his books that he had several books on the Vedas themselves. This aroused my interest in the Vedas and I ordered these books and studied them with great interest, meditating carefully upon them, including *Secret of the Veda* and *Hymns to the Mystic Fire.*

My encounters with the Vedas through these books were not mere intellectual experiences. They represented a contact with the Divine Word, Vak or the Divine Speech, the Goddess Sarasvati. I felt the presence of the Vedic Dawn, like the Dawn of humanity, the beginning of creation, and the building of a new world for the Divine. This began my study of the Vedas, which was rooted in poetry with a background of Vedanta.

Yet I was not completely satisfied in simply following Sri Aurobindo's interpretation. I wanted to know what the Vedic rishis themselves saw and felt. A few years later when I was twenty-seven, having gone through most of what was available in English on the Vedas, I decided to look at the Vedas and Upanishads in the original Sanskrit. As there were no teachers available to me, as I was then living in a remote town in Northern California, I started with the Sanskrit texts and a Sanskrit grammar book and began trying to figure out the language myself, starting with the oldest Rig Veda itself. It was a rather unusual and haphazard way to learn Sanskrit, starting with the most difficult and oldest part of the language, but somehow it worked.

The Vedic language gradually unfolded its meaning through a study of the images, sounds and roots upon which the language was based. I felt an inner affinity with the teaching so that I did not find the texts to be difficult, though the grammar was often cumbersome. I soon discovered that the interpretations generally accepted for the older Vedas—not only those done by modern Western scholars but the traditional school of Sayana—as Aurobindo had noted, were indeed limited if not erroneous. The result of this research was that I produced a book on the Upanishads and the Vedas called the *Creative Vision of the Early Upanishads*. It traced back the Vedantic teaching of the universal Self found in the Upanishads to an origin in an earlier and more powerful Vedic vision. This was opposite the way it is usually explained, which is to view the Upanishads as exalted philosophy developing from a crude Vedic ritualistic base.

A friend of mine, who had recently become a disciple of M.P. Pandit, a noted yogi, author and secretary of the Sri Aurobindo Ashram, recommended that I visit Pandit during an upcoming trip of his to the United States. I knew that if anyone would understand what I was doing it would be him, as Pandit had done many books on the Vedas and Upanishads, with similar ideas. I explained my views to him that the Vedas contained a science of Self-realization hidden in their teaching, from their very first mantra to the Divine Fire (Agni). He was happy to know of my work and told me that he would help publish it in India. He encouraged me to follow out my studies, which he explained was a kind of Divine mission given to me.

I told him that I was not academically trained, nor had I yet studied in India, and that my work was merely personal and never intended for publication. I said that I did not feel qualified to comment on the Vedas in a public way. He replied that it was good that I wasn't academically trained, that it gave me a direct and independent insight, so that I would not just merely repeat the same errors as other scholars. He told me to trust my vision.

If I had such insights and had produced such work it was for a greater purpose and should not be limited to my own private study.

Naturally this moved me to continue my Vedic work with more effort and dedication. I worked on the Rig Veda itself and in four months had produced a five hundred page book on the Vedas, which I mailed to Pandit and he began serializing it in *World Union* and later other publications of the Sri Aurobindo Ashram in 1980.

I began sending articles out to other publications in India as well, including to the ashram publications of Ramana Maharshi and Anandamayi Ma, as well as to Motilal Banarsidass, the main publisher of Indological books. These articles were almost invariably published, which additionally encouraged me to go further. Thus my Vedic work began and developed spontaneously and independently. I sort of naturally fell into it. I never had a plan to do so. And in retrospect it would appear to be a ludicrous thing to attempt, particularly by someone at my age and background working largely on his own.

After developing this foundation I gained many contacts and much support for my work throughout the world, though it took over ten years to get it recognized in a broader way. I have since taken many trips to India and studied and discussed the Vedas with many teachers, which would require a number of separate stories to relate. I have worked with Ayurveda and Vedic astrology as well, expanding the range of my original Vedic research. Later I found many of the same ideas and inspirations of my studies in the works of Ganapati Muni, who was perhaps the chief disciple of Ramana Maharshi. But the basic core of my Vedic views has not changed. In India I experienced the Vedic vision not only in the people but in the temples and the landscape of both the North and South of the country. I also learned traditional Vedic chanting which opened up another level of the teaching for me. I came into contact with a number of great teachers both known and unknown in the West.

What was it that I discovered in the Vedas? What made the Vedas more important to me than other spiritual or intellectual teachings? It was not just philosophy or poetry of an exalted nature. Nor was it the later portion of the Vedas alone, the Upanishads that drew my interest but also the most ancient Rig Veda itself and its wealth of mantras and symbols. The Rig Veda for me is the doorway to the mind of the rishis, to the cosmic mind itself, the very heart of creation. The Vedic vision is a universal mantric knowledge that integrates all aspects of human knowledge including yoga, philosophy, poetry, psychology, mythology and ritual. The Vedas are like an ongoing explosion of insights, with every sort of color and form, merging ultimately into a pure lightning illumination that has no end.

For me the Vedas are a living teaching and the Vedic rishis are living teachers. There is no gap of time or culture between those of us who live today and the Vedas of many thousands of years past. The Vedas transcend time. Nor do I see the Vedas as merely Indian or Hindu, they are the heritage of the greater spiritual humanity from which we have fallen and to which we must return. The Vedas are part of each one of us by the very fact that we are human beings. The Vedas are part of us or, to be more accurate, we are part of the Vedas. They are the very fabric of the cosmic intelligence that works inside us and in all the universe upholding the great beauty and harmony of life.

The Vedas exist at the core of all real seeking to connect with Truth through the great forces of nature and consciousness, whether it is in the form of Native American, ancient Greek, Egyptian, or even modern scientific approaches. In that connecting to the universal Being and its powers lies the Vedas, and there the Vedas must eventually be found. The Vedas are not merely particular books—though the Vedic texts we do have are authentic—but are the very vibrations of the Divine Word, the Primal Sound, the voice of original Reality.

I don't find that most of the Vedic mantras are hard to understand, though some of them remain obscure to me today. What could be more obvious than the dawn and the sun that rises every day? Yet the dawn and the sun are not mere outer realities, they are outer symbols, intimations of an inner reality of enlightenment and illumination that is our true home. The Vedas are the language of Nature not as outer phenomena but as a poetry of the spirit, which is the real meaning and beauty of creation. To me what is hard to understand is not the Vedas but the modern world with its technology that alienates us from nature, its commercialism that warps our minds, its endless desires and sensations that keep us ever restless and disturbed, its artificial dogmas and ideologies which cloud our perception and divide us up into hostile camps, compared to which the Vedic world is indeed paradise.

The final answer as to my connection with the Vedas perhaps goes back to the truth of karma and rebirth. There is really no reason why a person of my background would take to this Vedic work and be able to get anywhere with it. The only answer is the samskaras, the impressions from previous births. This was a knowledge that came with me, that I was born with, the result of a previous life which I have since come to remember in various aspects. For example, when I received my first copies the Vedas in Sanskrit it was not something ancient or foreign that I saw but an old friend and companion.

Nor do I approach the Vedas from an academic or even personal perspective. To approach the Vedas I first put my mind into a silent state and let the teaching unfold itself without the interference of my own thoughts. This is not done through mental effort, though there is the effort of concentration. It is like opening an irrigation channel to a great river and letting the water come in. It occurs through turning the mind within.

The great beauty of the Hindu religion is that the impressions it creates within us remain with us life after life. It is not a religion limited to one life only, and its benefit carries through all of our lives to the final liberation of the soul. In this regard the impressions of the Vedas can be found in each one of us, if we know how to look deeply for them. While unusual, I don't think what I have experienced with the Vedas is unique. I think that many more people, East and West, will come to it in time. The Vedas are not only our most ancient past but the key to our global future as well. We are once more moving back toward the Vedic vision as our culture moves once more in a global and cosmic direction.

The message of my encounter with the Vedas to modern Hindus is this: Your spiritual tradition is perhaps the greatest treasure of all humanity. Please cherish it, sustain it, practice it and share it with all. Whatever deficiencies may be in India or Hindu culture economically or politically, should not get a person to forget the power of the Vedas. The Vedas are like the sun. In them is the key to all light, life and love for all the world, through which all problems, individual or collective, can be solved. Let us not forget our Vedic heritage and those who have access to Vedic knowledge, please study it and strive to preserve it.

Index